Praise for the \
Les and Leslie

"Les and Leslie are grounded, understandable, and immensely practical. They deal in the real world and offer real answers and solutions."
—Gary D. Chapman, author of *The Five Love Languages*

"With an incredible blend of contemporary social science and a deep understanding of Scripture, Les Parrott's writing will help you see beyond what you may be tempted to settle for. And he'll show you the way, step by step, to realizing the kinds of relationships we all long for."
—Lee Strobel, *New York Times* bestselling author

"The Parrotts' message is so valuable in helping you find real and dependable applications for emotional health."
—Henry Cloud, coauthor of *Boundaries*

"Refreshingly honest and incredibly practical."
—Lysa TerKeurst, president of Proverbs 31 and
New York Times bestselling author

"Challenging, real-life application that will truly make a difference in the way you interact with the people around you."
—Craig Groeschel, pastor of Life.Church
and author of *Divine Direction*

"Don't miss out on the Parrotts' message. . . . It will truly transform your relationships."
—Christine Caine, founder of A21 and Propel Women

"Will positively change the way you interact with everyone."
—Dr. David Jeremiah, founder and president
of Turning Point and senior pastor of Shadow
Mountain Community Church in El Cajon, CA

"You can always count on Drs. Parrott to be rich in research and learnable in practice."

—Dr. John Townsend, author and speaker

"Practical sometimes means pat. For the Parrotts, it means genuinely helpful."

—Larry Crabb, bestselling author and counselor

"Les and Leslie are relationship experts who make eternal truths understandable and applicable."

—John C. Maxwell, *New York Times* bestselling author and leadership expert

"Nobody writes more clearly and with more insight on emotional health and relationships than Les and Leslie."

—Judah Smith, author of *Jesus is* _____

Healthy Me, Healthy Us

Also by Les and Leslie Parrott

Healthy Me, Healthy Us

Your Relationships Are Only
as Strong as You Are

DRS. LES AND LESLIE PARROTT

NELSON
BOOKS

An Imprint of Thomas Nelson

Published in Nashville, Tennessee, by Nelson Books, an imprint of Thomas Nelson. Nelson Books and Thomas Nelson are registered trademarks of HarperCollins Christian Publishing, Inc.

Published in association with Yates & Yates, www.yates2.com.

Thomas Nelson titles may be purchased in bulk for educational, business, fund-raising, or sales promotional use. For information, please e-mail SpecialMarkets@ThomasNelson.com.

ISBN 978-1-4002-0787-9 (eBook)
ISBN 978-1-4002-1025-1 (TP)

Library of Congress Cataloging-in-Publication Data

Names: Parrott, Les, author. | Parrott, Leslie L., 1964- author.
Title: Healthy me, healthy us : your relationships are only as strong as your are / Drs. Les and Leslie Parrott.
Description: Nashville, Tennessee : Nelson Books, 2020. | Includes bibliographical references. |
Summary: "#1 New York Times bestselling authors and renowned psychologists Drs. Les and Leslie Parrott share the single most important secret to happy relationships"-- Provided by publisher.
Identifiers: LCCN 2019049539 (print) | LCCN 2019049540 (ebook) | ISBN 9781400207855 (hardcover) | ISBN 9781400207862 (ebook)
Subjects: LCSH: Self-actualization--Religious aspects--Christianity.| Health--Religious aspects--Christianity. | Interpersonal relations--Religious aspects--Christianity.
Classification: LCC BV4598.2 .P365 2020 (print) | LCC BV4598.2 (ebook) | DDC 248.4--dc23
LC record available at https://lccn.loc.gov/2019049539
LC ebook record available at https://lccn.loc.gov/2019049540

To Ranjy and Shine Thomas:
Two of the happiest and healthiest people we
know—we are forever indebted to both of you.

Contents

Contents

A Deep and Simple Plan

Life is deep and simple, and what our society
gives us is shallow and complicated.

—FRED ROGERS

Relationships are rife with potential disappointment, conflict, and confusion. But make no mistake: relationships are also our number one source of happiness. Nothing else comes close. Success, wealth, or achievement can't take the place of fulfilling relationships. Especially close ones. Nothing else tugs as tight on our hearts or delights our spirits more than a relationship that meets our longing for belonging.

That's why we hear the same question over and over. We hear it on a near-daily basis. It could be a reporter writing a story, a blogger looking for insight, a radio host doing an interview, a college student in a class, or an attendee at one of our live events. In one form or another they all pose a question they think is being asked for the first time: *What's the single most important thing you can do for your relationships?*

It's a great question. We've thought about it, researched it, lectured on it, and written about it for more than twenty-five years. And as two psychologists specializing in relationships, we have whittled down our answer to two words: *get healthy*.

Of course, this deserves some unpacking. If you were to attend a lecture or a seminar with us, you might hear us sum it up in a longer sentence. In fact, this single sentence can revolutionize every relationship you ever attempt to build. Whether it's on the home front or with friends, whether it's in your love life or your work life, if you allow the truth of this single sentence to seep into the cortex of your brain and be lived out through your spirit, your relationships will never be the same. Here it is:

If you try to build intimacy with another before you have gotten whole on your own, all your relationships become an attempt to complete yourself.

And these relationships will fall flat. Guaranteed. Why? Because nobody was designed to complete you. Not a friend, colleague, family member, or even your soul mate. Nobody can do that work for you. Nobody in your life is a shortcut to personal wholeness. They can help you, as iron sharpens iron, but ultimately you are the one who must do the work on your own to become psychologically, emotionally, and spiritually whole. And when you do, your everything changes. Why? *Because your relationships can only be as healthy as you are.*

Did you catch that? This is key. It's the hinge upon which the entire message of this book hangs. If you want to have healthy relationships with other people, you've got to be healthy yourself. Your relationships don't necessarily need more skills, tips, or tactics—those have their place. What your relationships need most is something deeper, something stronger, something that has more to do with your *being* than your *doing*. Your relationships need emotional health.

You Are Meant for This

Few places on the planet are visited by more tourists than Florence, Italy. Like millions before us, we made the trip on a sweltering summer day to see the home of the Renaissance masters. Of course most people, including us, head straight to Michelangelo's large-scale sculpture of the biblical hero David. Carved from a single block of Carrara marble, the seventeen-foot figure was first unveiled more than

> Wholeness does not mean perfection: it means embracing brokenness as an integral part of life.
>
> —PARKER J. PALMER

five hundred years ago when Michelangelo was just twenty-six years old. This gleaming white marble masterpiece is said to be one of the most breathtaking pieces of art ever, modern or ancient.

We stood in line with thousands of others to see it. We took obligatory photos and marveled at the proportion, beauty, and detail of this world-famous statue. But then, wanting to escape the hordes of people gathered around the towering David, we wandered down the hall of the museum and found something even more compelling, if not less popular. Four unfinished statues. Huge chunks of marble with a hand protruding here, a torso of a man there, a leg, a part of a head. None was finished.

These fragmentary figures seemed to be crying out to break free from their blocks of marble. They were so close to becoming what they were intended to be. But they are *non-finito*. Michelangelo called these figures "the Captives." He believed that his work was simply revealing what was already within the stone. But in the case of these four pieces, the process of Michelangelo chipping away at the excess to reveal what was meant to be was never realized. It was cut short. And so the four figures stand there. Unfinished.

Study them for a time, and they are certain to stir within you a longing to be more complete yourself. They touch an ache in your own soul to be free from whatever is holding you down and preventing your full potential. The incomplete figures remind you of your *own* incompleteness.

All of us, as humans, share a universal longing to be complete and whole. We want to be all that God intended. But like Michelangelo's Captives, we are too often frozen in our efforts to experience who we are really meant to be. We never learn the secrets to chipping away at what holds us back. We never discover the parts of ourselves that are still in captivity. The result? We remain imprisoned by the unfinished work of becoming whole. And our relationships suffer.

Defining Your Destination

You may be single or married, young or old. You may live a charmed life or suffer unthinkable challenges. Whatever your baggage or background, we know at least one thing about you. Each moment of every day you are moving either away from or toward the person God designed you to be. As a result, either your inner self is deteriorating into something unattractive or it is quietly becoming a work of art. You are either maximizing your moments or allowing them to slip by without notice.

> I will no longer act on the outside in a way that contradicts the truth that I hold deeply inside. I will no longer act as if I were less than the whole person I know myself inwardly to be.
>
> —ROSA PARKS

No matter your age, stage, faith, or career, all of us, if we choose, are on a journey of wholeness. It's a process that never ends. Nobody checks this task off their to-dos. Nobody ever "arrives." We are all in process. But how do we know if we are making progress? It begins by understanding what we mean by being healthy and whole.

Let's make this clear: being healthy is not the same as being happy. But you can't be happy without being healthy. And there's a lot more to health than not being sick. Emotional health is more than the absence of dysfunctional emotions. Healthy people contend with depression, stress, anger, anxiety, and all the rest; but they don't let their feelings determine their destiny. They manage their emotions. They remain optimistic even during setbacks. They experience contentment, purpose, and meaning. They feel sure-footed and have an abundance of love for others. In other words, they have confidence in themselves as well as empathy for others.

The healthy person is far from perfect, however. In fact, they are the first to admit their shortcomings. They own their dark side, their ugly parts. They recognize and study their personal flaws, wounds, and idiosyncrasies. Knowing they have blind spots, they are on an unending quest for better self-insight. They're committed to seeing themselves truthfully. Authenticity is key. Not content to accept their shortcomings and limitations, they move toward growth. Improving is their passion. They use their pain to make progress, their hurts to heal. In fact, their brokenness and failures become the accelerant of their growth, not the deterrent. Health and healing walk together when we pursue wholeness. The whole person integrates the good and bad, the light and dark, the pain and healing.

In short, health and wholeness are a state of emotional well-being. Would you know it if you saw it? Here's a quick quality comparison of the healthy person versus the person who is struggling in their relationships.

Healthy	Unhealthy
Self-aware	Self-absorbed
Proactive	Reactive
Resilient	Inflexible
Optimistic	Pessimistic
Confident	Insecure
Empathic	Indifferent
Humble	Entitled
Grateful	Resentful
Growing	Passive

Of course, everyone is on a continuum when it comes to these qualities. You may even want to note where you think you land on each of these dimensions. For example, would you say you are more self-aware or self-absorbed? What would the people who know you best say? Would they agree with you? If you feel comfortable, review the list above and note which side of the continuum you fall on for each quality. Out of the nine qualities listed, circle the three you think need the most improvement in your life. Would your family and friends agree? If you're not game for this right now, that's okay. We have a more important suggestion later in this introduction.

It's Not Complicated—We Promise

"Life is deep and simple, and what our society gives us is shallow and complicated." Fred Rogers, the Mister Rogers of children's television, said this in a thoughtful interview shortly before he passed away. What a wise and compassionate man. And what an amazing and insightful sentence. Life *is* deep and simple. And yet we so often make it more complicated than it needs to be.

The scientific study of emotional health and wholeness is new, but the principles it excavates are ages old. How do we know? Because we've studied the pursuit of a life well lived from every vantage point, going far back into ancient history. The Greeks, for example, viewed the deep pleasures of life as being more of the mind than the body. Roman statesman Cicero proclaimed, "There is no fool who is happy, and no wise man who is not." Epicurus boiled fulfillment down to a straightforward thought: the most contented people remember the past with gratitude and accept their present situation without coveting what someone else has. The Bible says the same thing, in so many words, and then drills down on the point that true fulfillment comes ultimately through love—of ourselves, one another, and our Creator. Something about the truthful

> When we are not honest, . . . we are cut off from a significant resource of ourselves, a vital dimension that is necessary for unity and wholeness.
>
> —CLARK MOUSTAKAS

simplicity of this age-old wisdom got hold of our hearts as well as our heads as we set out to find a practical plan for helping all of us be the best versions of "whole" people we can be. We've grown weary of seeing people spend inordinate amounts of time and money in the pursuit of wholeness, whatever their route, only to feel more confused and aimless as a result. So let us tell you what we know for sure. After surveying history's pursuit of personal growth, and after studying contemporary science's study of well-being, we know that health and wholeness, like life itself, is deep and simple. Don't be seduced by turning it into something shallow or complicated.

So what is our deep and simple plan for helping you become healthier and more whole? It is a clear pathway for getting you from where you are to where you want to be.

An easy path? Not always. But simple nonetheless.

The Three Hallmarks of Health

Name any brand: Nike, Coca-Cola, FedEx, Colgate, Starbucks, Verizon, Tiffany. They all have trademarks, a registration of ownership. Trademarks protect brands from being copied by others. A hallmark, on the other hand, is a literal mark on a precious metal attesting to the material's quality and authenticity. It's not about a company's brand. It is about being tested and approved at the highest levels. To identify something as a *hallmark* means it is of outstanding quality.

That's the case with the three steps we offer in this book. They are proven and tested. They are hallmarks. Beginning in part one, each of the chapters will set you on a proven pathway for personal growth. Each of them will show you how to take a step forward.

What are these three steps? We call them the three hallmarks of health:

1. Profound significance
2. Unswerving authenticity
3. Self-giving love

These are the elements of health and wholeness boiled down to the basics. It's that simple. At the risk of sounding too colloquial on such a meaningful matter, you can also think of health and wholeness as *getting right with God* (significance), *getting right with yourself* (authenticity), and *getting right with others* (love). Simple? We hope so. But as you read more about these hallmarks, we think you will recognize just how profound they are.

Obviously, we don't take credit for inventing these hallmarks. We are attempting only to breathe new life into these ancient principles as we provide you with practical and proven strategies for living them out.

This definition of emotional and spiritual health and wholeness is as old as the ages and as fresh as contemporary research. Its simplicity can compel you to make it more complicated, but there's no need. The depth of these qualities, if properly understood, has been enough to propel the ultimate human quest throughout the ages.

These three hallmarks of health apply to everyone across cultures and over time. In fact, these hallmarks have been bandied about for centuries.

> You don't need another person, place, or thing to make you whole. God already did that. Your job is to know it.
>
> —MAYA ANGELOU

Speaking of the value of *significance*, for example, Augustine, in AD 391 said, "God loves each of us as if there were only one of us."

Speaking of *authenticity*, Jesus said to his followers, "What will it profit a man if he gains the whole world, and loses his own soul?" (Mark 8:36 NKJV).

And speaking of *self-giving love*, in 4 BC Seneca said, "If thou wishest to be loved, love."

In fact, long before social scientists studied the process for becoming emotionally healthy, the hallmarks of health were outlined in a letter the apostle Paul wrote to the Ephesians (3:14–19, 4:1–3):

- Profound Significance

  "I ask him that with both feet planted firmly on love, you'll be able to take in with all followers of Jesus the extravagant dimensions of Christ's love. Reach out and experience the breadth! Test its length! Plumb the depths! Rise to the heights! Live full lives, full in the fullness of God" (3:14–19).

- Unswerving Authenticity

  "I want you to get out there and walk—better yet, run!—on the road God called you to travel. I don't want any of you sitting around on your hands. I don't want anyone strolling off, down some path that goes nowhere" (4:1–2).

- Self-Giving Love

  "Pouring yourselves out for each other in acts of love, alert at noticing differences and quick at mending fences" (4:3).

Profound significance. Unswerving authenticity. Self-giving love. If you want to avoid what some call the "tragedy of being half-formed," like Michelangelo's Captives, and you want to become all that God designed you to be, these three hallmarks will open the door.

Will you be perfect? No.

Healthy? Yes.

You Can Do This (Really)

Since you are reading this book, we know that something within you has been stirred to move more intentionally toward personal health and wholeness. And we are going to do everything we can to help you experience it deeply and consistently.

We are going to help you get a lock on the hallmarks of health. But be forewarned. The positive results of this journey become evident in miniscule moments. They are not doled out in one lump sum. You won't complete this book and be done with it. This book will get you moving in a positive direction. At times you will excel. At other times you will grope. But instead of feeling discouraged, take comfort in the fact that you are groping in the right direction. That's how true and lasting growth occurs.

Another word of caution. *All three* hallmarks of health—significance, authenticity, and love—are *essential* for wholeness. They build on one another. And they stand like a tripod. If one leg is missing, wholeness topples. Consider the facts:

> Destiny is not a matter of chance, it is a matter of choice; it is not a thing to be waited for, it is a thing to be achieved.
> —WILLIAM JENNINGS BRYAN

- Without significance, you're insecure.
- Without authenticity, you're phony.
- Without love, you're indifferent.

The point is that unhealthy people, by default, suffer from varying degrees of being anxious, superficial, and egocentric. Like Michelangelo's Captives, they are developed in places but conspicuously incomplete.

Does insecurity sometimes get the better of you? Are

you sometimes more concerned with how you are seen than with being who you are? Do you sometimes allow your self-centered motives to drive you more than you'd like? You are not alone. And you're certainly not doomed. You don't have to be captive. You can decide to step out on your pathway toward wholeness—guided by significance, authenticity, and love. It is the most important choice you will ever make for your relationships (and for yourself), ultimately enabling your longing for belonging to be fulfilled at the deepest levels.

Getting Healthy and Whole Is Your Choice

"I never knew I had a choice."

It's the saddest sentence we ever hear in our counseling offices. Many things in life are beyond our control—our eye color, our race, the hurricane on the East Coast. But there is a vast, unclaimed territory of actions over which we have a major say. These actions involve the countless choices we make—or don't make—every day, concerning how we lead our lives. Unfortunately, many people cede control to others or leave these choices to fate.

"Nothing I do matters," we often hear them say. Or "I've tried everything, and it doesn't help." They shift responsibility to everything and everyone. They eventually settle for what is and dare not think of what could be. All because they didn't make choices.

In a very simple experiment, psychologists Ellen Langer

of Harvard and Judith Rodin of Yale clearly demonstrated the beneficial effects of making choices. They gave a group of nursing home residents potted plants to care for. In addition to giving them responsibility for the little plants, they also offered the residents suggestions on doing more for themselves, making their own decisions instead of letting the staff do that for them. A second group, matched with the first in terms of their degree of ill health or disability, received the usual nursing home treatment with the staff announcing that they would be responsible for the residents' care, making all the decisions for them.

Within just three weeks, the first group showed significant improvement in heath and activity. Even more dramatic were the results after eighteen months. The death rate of the group who were encouraged to make their own decisions was *half* that of the other group.

Another study at the University of Washington found that depression and anxiety were high among students who believed they had little or no control over what happened to them. Those who perceived themselves as being in charge of their lives showed no depression or anxiety despite high stress.

We could fill this book with hundreds of studies demonstrating

> The difficulty in life is the choice.
> —GEORGE MOORE

the positive impact of self-responsibility and choice. In the professional literature it's called "self-efficacy." However you label it, you can be certain that your path to becoming healthy and whole is predicated on your choice to take the steps we're about to show you.

So if you are the kind of person who sometimes starts but doesn't finish, here's our challenge: make a decision, right now, to follow through on your intention to read the chapters of this book. Set goals, along with a timeline, of when you will have these chapters read. You won't read them by accident. You'll read them—and practice what you learn—when you make a choice to do so.

Two Suggestions

We are eager for you to jump into part one of this book, but before you do, we have a couple of practical suggestions. First, consider going through this book with someone else. Or better yet, with a small group (even after you read it on your own). Why? Because when you process information like this with other people, you are sure to better internalize it yourself. We've developed additional resources for just this purpose. If you want to learn more, go to HealthyMeHealthyUs.com.

One other suggestion: this one has to do with helping you become more self-aware, right at the start. This book is ultimately about your relationships—making them stronger and more fulfilling. And it's based on you knowing yourself better.

Self-awareness is arguably the most fundamental and essential place for beginning the journey of self-growth and well-being. Why? Because you can't work on something if you're not aware of it. Awareness is curative. It's the prerequisite to health and wholeness.

You can read everything we have to say about profound significance, unswerving authenticity, and self-giving love. But if you can't see how these three steps apply to you, it won't matter.

For this reason, we suggest you invest in a personality tool—a virtual mirror for helping you see *you* better. Of course, there are numerous ways to do this, and you've probably taken several self-assessments at various points in your life. But if you want to experience the one we've built for just this purpose, visit Yada.com.

Our Yada Assessment takes fifteen minutes to answer a few questions online, and it will immediately provide you with a custom report all about you. Don't worry. You won't get graded. It's not about being evaluated. It's about increasing your self-awareness. It highlights your personality—how you are hardwired. And it explores your talk style, your conflict quotient, your resiliency factor, and much more. By the way, the term

> It is not enough to stare up the steps—we must step up the stairs.
>
> —VANCE HAVNER

yada is a Hebrew word (used nearly a thousand times in the Bible) that means "to know." The Yada Assessment is all about *knowing* you, *knowing* others, and being *known* by others. Of course, taking this assessment is merely a suggestion. It's not a requirement for reading this book. You can discover more about it at the website.

Invest Wisely

"People are anxious to improve their circumstances," said author James Allen, "but are unwilling to improve themselves." That's often true. But not for you. You wouldn't be reading these words if that were the case. You are already intentional about getting started on this journey. But keep in mind that intentions aren't good enough. Imagine the world we'd live in if everyone did what they intended to do!

Don't make the mistake of putting this off. You and your relationships deserve to be the best they can be. Make a commitment right now to dig into part one of the book. You'll have plenty of distractions and interruptions. But don't let them sabotage your good intentions. Follow through.

"Your life is like a coin," said Lillian Dickson. "You can spend it any way you like, but you can spend it only once." The question is, how are you going to spend your capital? It is a question we explore personally and thoroughly in this book, and, because you are reading it, we know you want to make the very best investment you can. We're going to make it easy for you. You're going to discover a map to wholeness. It will show you the pathway to well-being and what steps to take to make sure you get an incredible return on your investment. We've seen countless people choose to put the hallmarks of significance, authenticity, and love to work in their own lives, and they have thriving relationships to prove it.

Everyone has a longing for belonging. We are designed for relationship. But before that need can be truly fulfilled, we must first address our *compulsion for completion.*

We'll be pulling for you every step of the way.

LES AND LESLIE PARROTT
SEATTLE, WASHINGTON

PART ONE

Profound Significance

*God loves each of us as if
there were only one of us.*

—SAINT AUGUSTINE

> *I ask him that with both feet planted firmly on love, you'll be able to take in with all followers of Jesus the extravagant dimensions of Christ's love. Reach out and experience the breadth! Test its length! Plumb the depths! Rise to the heights! Live full lives, full in the fullness of God. . . .*

I want you to get out there and walk—better yet, run!—on the road God called you to travel. I don't want any of you sitting around on your hands. I don't want anyone strolling off, down some path that goes nowhere. . . .

Pouring yourselves out for each other in acts of love, alert at noticing differences and quick at mending fences.

Ephesians 3:14–19; 4:1–3

We had just stepped onto the platform in the Rose Garden Arena in Portland, Oregon, where nearly ten thousand people had assembled for a mega marriage seminar. That night each of the six speakers was to give a brief overview of what we would be speaking on over the next couple of days. Just before the rest of us went to the podium, our friend Gary Smalley captivated the crowd by holding up a crisp fifty-dollar bill and asking the massive audience, "Who would like this fifty-dollar bill?" Hands started going up everywhere. He said, "I am going to give this fifty dollars to one of you, but first let me do this." He proceeded to crumple up the bill. Then he asked, "Who still wants it?" The same hands went up in the air.

"Well," he replied, "what if I do this?" He dropped it on the ground and started to grind it into the floor with his shoe. He picked it up, all crumpled and dirty. "Now who still wants it?" Again, hands went into the air. "You have all learned a valuable lesson," Gary said. "No matter what I do to the money, you still want it because it doesn't decrease in value. It is still worth fifty dollars."

Gary's simple illustration underscores a profound point. Many times in our lives we are dropped, crumpled, and ground into the dirt by the decisions we make or the circumstances that come our way. We may feel worthless, insignificant in our own and in others' eyes. But no matter what has happened or what will happen, we never lose our value if we choose to accept our significance.

Perhaps you've already internalized the message that crowd in Portland heard, and you already have a profound sense of significance. Maybe you already know at the center of your being, deep down in your soul, that your value is established for all time. Your *lovability*, and thus your significance, is rooted deep in God's unending love for you. You don't have to work harder, look better, or win prizes of any kind. You know and live the most crucial message ever articulated: that you have inestimable worth because you are a creation of the Creator.

Chances are, however, that even if you have experienced this significance at *some* time, you don't feel significant *all* the time. Research reveals that while many of us have heard this ancient truth about our worth, most of us, most of the time, don't incorporate it into our everyday lives. It doesn't really make a difference. We hear the message. We agree with it. And that's that. But instead of being confident of our significance—feeling it resonate deep within our bones every day—we fall back into the habit of trying to earn it. Even if we agree that our Creator loves us, we still end up feeling better about ourselves only when we are winning the attention and approval of others.

We seem to be on a cosmic quest to *establish* our value—to prove it, earn it, deserve it—so we can *somehow* experience the ultimate feeling of inner well-being. And once we find what we're looking for, we relax—but only momentarily. Eventually the people we are pleasing—whether a parent, a spouse, a friend, an advisory board, or an audience—quit sending us love messages. Ultimately, we find ourselves back on our endless quest.

Finding the love of your life, for example, is an incredible experience, but it will not ultimately quench your thirst for significance. Neither will having children, as miraculous as that experience is. And neither will becoming famous, writing a bestseller, or building a successful company. Still, we run helter-skelter, always restless, desperate to find that next person, thing, or event that will satisfy our search. No wonder so many of us can identify with King Solomon's words: "Everything was meaningless, a chasing after the wind" (Eccl. 2:11 NIV).

In our clinical work, we are astounded and saddened that the majority of individuals we work with never experience their own deep sense of significance. It doesn't seem to matter how much they believe a set of doctrines, subscribe to a particular faith, or even share their truth with others. The fact is, they feel good about themselves when they *do* important things, *win* important promotions or prizes, *please* the crucial people, and thus *earn* the right to see themselves in a positive light. As soon as they quit doing, winning, pleasing, and earning, they feel awful about themselves.

You may, at times, feel positive about yourself. But if that feeling of significance comes and goes, and then you're back on the treadmill of *doing*, you haven't yet grasped your true worth. And you're not alone. The most common addiction of all, we've found, is the endless internal compulsion to satisfy your frantic quest to feel good about yourself by simply making yourself worthy of positive self-assessments. In other words, you've fallen for the "you have to *do* something in order to *be* someone" trap. You feel you must lose weight, climb the corporate ladder, birth a child, make a certain amount of money, or become a leader to gain significance.

But a deep sense of personal significance doesn't depend on externals. And it's foundational to emotional health. Until you claim this significance at your core, you cannot be emotionally whole. When you try to earn this significance and assume you deserve it because of your "success," you will only gain an artificial and worthless variety of it. Such a gain really contributes *nothing* to your overall emotional health. In fact, it may well blind you to the fact that you don't feel intrinsically good about being you.

Why is it so hard to embrace the fact that profound personal significance is received, not achieved? Why are we so addicted to trying to prove our value? These questions have haunted the human race for centuries. Part of the answer, we believe, is that we are rarely given the tools to receive this truth in the deepest and most central parts of our beings—and this is exactly what we dedicate the next two chapters of this book to doing.

We want you to have the time-tested tools for *really* embracing your personal significance. Whether you are starting from the ground up or are already well on your way, we want to show you exactly how to receive the greatest love of your life. It is the most important and foundational step to wholeness, and it is key to helping you enjoy the kinds of relationships you long for.

The first chapter of this book explores self-talk. Without profound significance, you will be seduced by a cycle that is sure to leave you breathless. No matter how great the level of success, popularity, or power you achieve, the attention it garners will cause you to believe that whatever love has come your way is the result of what you do—not who you are. And you'll soon—inevitably—find yourself back where you started. Only this time little voices, "self-talk," will conspire to keep you feeling anxious. However good you feel about yourself when you have achieved that good feeling, you are only a whisper away from feeling bad. When your work is criticized, your sense of value is directly affected. When you're left alone or abandoned, you'll see such situations as evidence of your worthlessness. Instead of trying to understand your limitations when you fall short, you'll blame yourself, ironically, not for what you *did*, but for who you *are*.

Feelings of inferiority make little distinction between who you are and what you do. And when you lack a profound sense of significance, you will spend at least half your time feeling inferior. Fundamentally, though, whether you feel momentarily good or bad, anxiety will haunt your life. You will never be far from despair.

But that doesn't have to be the life you choose. You *can* have a life of profound significance. It begins with tuning in to the single most important conversation you ever have, your "self-talk." Your internal dialogue is key to learning exactly how you feel about you. It is an indispensable tool in learning to let love capture your being. What you say to yourself is the most important conversation you have all day. Yet precious few pay attention to it. And only the most well adjusted know how to monitor their inner voice for the sake of accepting their own significance. We dedicate the first chapter in this part to helping you tune in to your self-talk.

The second chapter helps you take a good look at your past—the factors that have shaped you. Why? Because this is the biggest obstacle to anyone wanting to embrace their significance. Pain from the past, for example, can keep some of us so stuck that we stay there forever. That's why, in chapter 2 of this section, we help you unpack your emotional baggage. You will be amazed by how the step-by-step exercises in this chapter can help you get unstuck and move more quickly than you imagined on your journey of personal growth. So get ready. We are going to help you identify any personal obstacles from your own history, and then get you moving on—beyond whatever may be holding you down from your past.

We'll say it again. Personal significance is the first time-tested step to health and wholeness. It is the prerequisite to well-being. You can never live to the fullest, never enjoy relationships at their peak, until you experience a permanent and profound sense of significance deep in the core of your being. Only then will you hear a voice that reverberates in every corner of your personality, saying, *I've known you from the beginning and called you by name. I knitted you together in your mother's womb and counted every hair on your head. Wherever you go, I go with you, and I'll never abandon you or hide my face from you. You belong to me, and I belong to you.*

You are marked by my love, and you are the pride of my life.
Nothing will ever separate us (Jer. 1:5).

When we experience this kind of love, when we recognize how profoundly significant we are to God, it opens the door to a full life. Ultimately, our compulsion for completion can only be met in God's love. When we experience this extravagant love from God *all* the time, it takes the pressure off our earthly relationships, empowering emotional intelligence and health with everyone we encounter.

ONE

Tuning In to Your Self-Talk

Thinking is the talking of the soul with itself.

—PLATO

If you bugged yourself, what would you hear?

Can you imagine having an internal recorder that could replay what you say when no one else is listening? What would it do for you to come home at the end of the day and download the recordings of conversations you had with yourself over the last several hours? What phrases would you hear more than once? Would your self-statements be positive or negative? And if you could do such a thing, what would listening to these internal tapes teach you?

First, you would almost certainly be surprised, maybe even shocked, if you listened in. The fact is, most of the time you have little conscious awareness of your own internal dialogue. Yet this "self-talk" has a huge impact on how you feel about yourself. It is the single most important determiner of whether you feel loved, respected, appreciated—significant.

For example, imagine you're on your way home at the end of a long day. You can't stop thinking about a painful conversation you had with a colleague. The whole scene flashes before you again. A couple of sharply worded comments fly from your mouth, and your colleague's face gets red, her eyes fill with tears, and her voice grows soft and quiet. She's genuinely hurt, and she doesn't know how to handle what you said. It bothers you all the way home. You feel embarrassed. Even guilty.

What was going on with you? Let's rerun your internal tape to find out.

Put yourself back in the lunchroom, back in the middle of the conversation. Listen in to what you were saying to yourself: *This conversation isn't going very well. I don't think she respects me. I've got to straighten her out before I lose more of her respect.*

This is why your words came out so fast, so sharply. If you could have been more conscious of this internal dialogue in that moment, you would have responded in a way that wouldn't have left you feeling embarrassed and guilty.

Here's the good news. Scientifically speaking, you *can* bug your own inner conversations. You can listen in to your internal dialogue as it is happening. Most important, you can use it to uncover your profound significance.

The Source of Your Significance

We'll say it straight out: The only sure way of getting a lock on your profound significance is to *receive* it—not *achieve* it. And the only place to receive the kind of love that infuses your being with this kind of perpetual significance is from God. Why? Because God is love (1 John 4:8). Period. God's love is not a reward. It's a gift. It has no contingencies. No clauses. No performance requirements. Paul says it this way: "God demonstrates his own love for us in this: While we were still sinners, Christ died for us" (Rom. 5:8 NIV). God doesn't withhold love until we shape up. He starts with love.

> What one thinks and talks about to himself tends to become the deciding influences in his life.
>
> —SIDNEY MADWED

In a world so committed to the idea that self-worth is a consequence of achievement or performance, this idea of love being a gift that merely needs to be accepted is difficult to maintain. Our challenge comes in truly receiving God's love, moment by moment, day by day. It's tough to wrap our minds around this kind of love, let alone experience it, because it's unconditional. You can't measure it. You can't quantify it. This love is extravagant. Always. That's why Paul, in his message to the Ephesians, issues a challenge: "to grasp how wide and long and high and deep is the love of Christ, and to know this love that surpasses knowledge—that you may be filled to the measure of all the fullness of God" (Eph. 3:18–19 NIV). Or in the words of *The Message*:

> I ask him that with both feet planted firmly on love,
> you'll be able to take in with all followers of Jesus
> the extravagant dimensions of Christ's love.
> Reach out and experience the breadth!
> Test its length!
> Plumb the depths!
> Rise to the heights!
> Live full lives, full in the fullness of God.

Until we accept this gift and experience it deep down in our bones, we will forever give in to the temptation of basing our self-worth on what we do instead of whose we are. That's where your self-talk comes in. We need to rewire our brains for the kind of self-talk that underscores this gift of love from God. We need to reprogram our inner dialogue.

Healthy people are keenly aware of what they say to themselves, how they say it, and when they say it. Moreover, they know that tuning in to self-talk unlocks the secret to experiencing their

> I came so they can have real and eternal life, more and better life than they ever dreamed of.
>
> —JESUS, IN JOHN 10:10

profound significance. Healthy people use rational self-talk as their passport to strong relationships.

Where Does Your Self-Talk Start?

On the campus of UCLA, in the Gonda Neuroscience and Genetics Research Center, is the Brain Research Institute (BRI). It houses laboratories where some of the world's most renowned neuroscientists do brain research. And according to its former director, the late Dr. Carmine Clemente, its central mission involves one of the most fascinating tasks in the world—to train the human brain to scrutinize itself. The BRI attempts to use intelligence for understanding the workings of the human mind. As they put it, "The human mind is what the brain does." So they study the brain to understand the mind.

It is a formidable undertaking. Not even the universe, with its countless billions of galaxies, represents greater wonder or complexity than the human brain. Consider this fact: if the brain of an average fifty-year-old could be fully emptied of all the impressions and memories it has stored, and they could be put on a list, the length of the list would reach to the moon and back several times! Truth be told, the contents of the human brain could never be fully inventoried or identified. The neurons of the human brain make the silicon chips and semiconductors that are hailed as supreme technological achievements look like child's play.

As recently as 1950, brain researchers thought they were

being extravagant when they guessed there might be as many as a billion neurons in the brain. Today the estimate is 86 billion. These neurons carry the traffic for millions of signals. As you read the words on this page, your brain sets off millions of electrochemical reactions to accurately understand and assimilate the information. When you visualize the face of a friend or recall what you had for lunch yesterday, the same process occurs. In short, numberless signals are flashing every second of our waking hours.

The brain is the only organ of the body that's totally essential for individual identity. If you have a defective kidney, liver, or heart, you can acquire a transplant and still retain your sense of self. But if you were to acquire a new brain, you would acquire a new personality. You would have a different set of memories, a different vocabulary, different aspirations. You'd also experience different emotions. A new way of thinking as well as feeling. With a new brain you would acquire a new mind. In short, assuming that medical science could solve the incredibly complex problems involved in a brain transplant, you would be somebody else in the same skin.

Clearly the power of the human brain is unmistakable. It does nothing less than preside over who you are.

And that is precisely why self-talk—what you say to yourself and how you interpret that inner

> I think, therefore I am.
>
> —DESCARTES

dialogue—is paramount to personal growth and well-being. Self-talk not only originates in the mind; it could be argued that the human mind *is* self-talk. At the risk of oversimplifying the majesty of the mind, you can think of it as a composition of intricate internal conversations. The brain is a circuitry of complex communication, relaying millions of messages at any moment. And these messages determine who you are. They have a direct impact not only on your body but on your psyche and your spirit as well. Your very personality is defined by your internal messages.

Your psychological state—whether confident and hopeful or insecure and cynical—is played out through a series of electrochemical connections in your brain that determine your mental state. In other words, *you* prescribe, to a large degree, what your brain does by what you say when no one's listening. And, over time, the secret messages you shoot repeatedly through your mind begin to cut a groove or wear a path through your cortex. The routine and habitual nature of these messages make them prominent, so they achieve a higher priority than other messages. These governing messages, the ones that are heard the loudest, most often, and quickest, are the ones that define your self-talk. These are the messages in your mind that we are about to examine, understand, and influence in this chapter.

What Is Self-Talk?

On a downtown bus, just as it is pulling in to its next stop, a woman stands up, slaps the face of the man next to her, and hurries to the exit. Each passenger who saw what happened reacts in their own way. A middle-aged man feels sad for the man who was slapped. A younger woman is frightened. A teenage boy is angry. Another woman feels excited. How could the same event trigger such an array of varying emotions? The answer is found in self-talk.

> The middle-aged man who reacted with sadness thought to himself, *He's lost her, and he'll never get her back.*
> The fearful woman thought, *She is really going to pay a price for that tonight when he sees her at home.*
> The angry teenager says to himself, *She humiliated him; she must be a real jerk.*
> The woman who felt excited said to herself, *Serves him right. What a strong woman; I wish I was more like that.*

In each case the event was almost instantaneously interpreted, judged, and labeled. And each individual's unique self-explanation resulted in a distinctive emotional experience— sadness, fear, anger, or excitement. The truth is, the emotional consequence of an event like this varies as much as the people observing it.

Each of us, every minute of every hour, holds an unending dialogue with ourselves, a dialogue that colors every experience. You could compare this dialogue to a waterfall of thoughts cascading down the back of your mind. The thoughts are rarely noticed, but they continually shape your attitudes, emotions, and outlook.

Self-talk is typically not spoken aloud, but its message is more piercing than any audible voice. What's more, it is reflexive. Automatic. Self-talk occurs without any prior reflection or reasoning, yet your brain instantly sees it as plausible and valid. That means your self-talk need not be accurate. In fact, for many of us it rarely is. But that doesn't hinder the mind from acting as if it were.

> It is very obvious that we are not influenced by "facts" but by our interpretation of the facts.
>
> —ALFRED ADLER

In 1955 a little-known professor of psychology at Rutgers University was building a counseling practice. But he was also growing increasingly disillusioned with the traditional methods of treatment. Psychoanalysis, in his opinion, was too costly, too long, and too out of touch with how people change. So he gave up psychoanalysis entirely and began his own brand of therapy with the founding of his Institute for Rational Living. Albert Ellis (1913–2007) was the first to use the term *self-talk*.

What does the term mean?

Self-talk is personal and specific.

Thomas, a college senior, has been sitting next to Tina in their English Literature class all semester. And all semester Thomas has entertained thoughts of asking her out. On several occasions he has started to do just that but is soon stopped in his tracks. *She doesn't want to go out with me*, he says to himself. And that puts an end to his efforts. Notice that Thomas is not saying, *Women are intimidating*, or even, *Tina doesn't like going out*. He is zeroing in on one specific thought that relates to him: *Tina doesn't want to go out with me*.

Self-talk is concise.

It is often composed of just a few words or even a brief visual image. Just two words—*Chico Way*—immediately engender inadequacy in me when I (Les) slip them into the crevices of my cortex. They tie into a miserable property decision I made several years ago that eventually cost me a hefty financial price. It was one of the worst decisions I have ever made. Up to that point I had thought I was pretty good at making important decisions . . . until *Chico Way* shattered my confidence. And since then, when I am in the throes of a significant decision, such as how to invest money, those two words, *Chico Way*, creep up on me and immediately pull me down.

> Feelings are simply what we say to ourselves about our experiences.
>
> —CHARLES T. BROWN

That's the nature of self-talk. It's concise. One word or a short phrase becomes shorthand for a group of self-reproaches, fears, or memories. And not one of us is immune to its power.

Self-talk is quick and spontaneous.

While waiting at a red light, you see a woman struggling to open the front door to an apartment while holding a baby in one arm and a bag of groceries in the other. At that very moment you see a man in a tailored suit walk right past her without even giving her a glance, let alone a helping hand. You quickly think, *Typical rich guy, not caring for anyone but himself.* The judgment is as real to you as your visual impression. When the light turns green, you're on your way. What you don't see is that the "rich guy" is completely blind. But after passing the woman, he hears the baby's cry and returns to offer help as best he can.

It's the nature of self-talk to waste no time in rushing to judgment.

Self-talk is believed, no matter how irrational.

We both do a great deal of public speaking and more than once have shared the same platform with other speakers at a major arena event with thousands in the audience. This experience is always charged with eager excitement and anticipation. Backstage, there's a lot of laughter, prayer, encouragement, and a fair degree of nervous energy. Once the event is over and the speaker team is in a van headed to the airport, the predictable question eventually emerges: "So, how do you think it went?" That's when every professional speaker analyzes everything from the audience response to the temperature of the arena. The outline of the program is picked over, and the timing of our jokes is evaluated. And if any speaker is feeling insecure, this is when it shows.

"I really missed the mark today," a speaker might say out loud. Of course, we counter the comment with a heavy dose of praise. But if the speaker believes his own self-talk (*I did a terrible job*), praise will do little good. He could have received a standing ovation from thousands, but if he feels he didn't meet his own standards, he genuinely thinks he's failed.

Irrational? You bet. But that's self-talk.

To sum up, self-talk, the automatic thoughts that cut a groove in our brains, is personal, specific, concise, quick, spontaneous, and believed.

Why Self-Talk Matters

Take a few minutes to press the rewind button on your mental tape player. Review a conversation you had with someone today. It may have been early this morning, as your two-year-old woke you up from a sound sleep. Or it could have been as you arrived at work. Perhaps it was over lunch with a friend or during a family dinner. Replay as much of the conversation as you can. Take a moment to do that right now.

> We act upon our thoughts. These thoughts literally become our daily life experience.
>
> —WAYNE DYER

Now rewind your mental recording to review the messages you sent yourself during that same interchange. Did those inner conversations come to mind as readily? Not if you are like most people. Most of us recall far more clearly the words we speak aloud than the words we speak to ourselves. So does that make our "outward dialogue" more important and lasting than our "inner dialogue"?

Consider the facts. Approximately 70 percent of our waking day is spent in one or more types of communication. Research suggests that you talk privately to yourself, however, at the rate of 400 to 4,000 words per minute. And this internal conversation is never turned off; it runs even while you sleep, monitoring your thoughts and feelings of significance and also influencing your hopes and dreams. Your self-talk is forming *who you are*.

We are constantly feeding our brains with information. Most of it is reflexive—messages that coordinate our muscles to walk or reach for a pen, for example. And then there is the self-talk that serves our daily activities, like *I need to stop at the cleaners*. But the self-talk that influences our psychological state is just as plentiful. At any given moment we say things to ourselves in rapid-fire succession that affect our well-being—our emotions, our energy level, our optimism or pessimism. Our self-talk can be positive or negative:

Positive Self-Talk	Negative Self-Talk
Optimistic: *I think I can do this.*	Pessimistic: *I can never do this.*
Rational: *Even competent people make mistakes.*	Irrational: *If I make a mistake, it means I'm incompetent.*
Internal Control: *I can influence my environment.*	External Control: *It all comes down to luck.*
Problems Are a Challenge: *I just need some time to figure this out.*	Problems Are a Threat: *It's simply impossible.*

Healthy Me, Healthy Us

The Undeniable Power of Self-Talk

If you want proof that self-talk matters, look no further than the placebo effect. It definitively shows that what we say to ourselves holds unbridled power. Abundant medical research has proven that what we think commands the brain to produce unassailable changes in the body's chemistry, setting the stage for either intensified illness or quicker recovery. So it stands to reason that if what we say in our brains can influence our bodies, what we say in our brains can affect our souls as well. If our self-talk impacts our physical well-being, in other words, imagine how it affects our emotional health, our feelings of significance.

You need not imagine it at all. The impact of self-talk on our emotions has been studied for decades from every angle, researched across cultures, and documented in countless scholarly journals and numerous professional presentations. A mountain of research has shown us that what you say to yourself, and how you explain and interpret the world around you, creates your emotional state. In a very real sense, *what you say and think to yourself becomes what you feel*.

Imagine walking along a jungle path at twilight and hearing a lion roar. Your muscles

> The first order of business of anyone who wants to enjoy success in all areas of his or her life is to take charge of the internal dialogue.
>
> —SIDNEY MADWED

tense, a knot forms in your stomach, and you can taste the fear rising in your throat. Why? Because, in a split second, you said something to this effect: *I'm in extreme danger. I could be attacked by a lion!* This self-talk not only set up a series of biological responses; it created fright and even panic.

Now imagine walking along a path at the San Diego Zoo at the same time of the evening and hearing the same sound. This time, of course, you barely flinch. Why? Because, in a split second, you said to yourself, *There's no cause for alarm. The lion is secured in his own cage.* The same stimulus, the roar, elicits very different emotional responses because of your self-talk.

This is all well and good, you may be saying, *but what difference does this make in my desire to become a more psychologically whole person?* We're glad you asked. Healthy people have learned how to harness the power of self-talk to control and manage their emotions, stay in contact with reality, focus their intentions, and optimize their potential. How? It begins by assessing just what your self-talk is saying.

Assessing Your Self-Talk

You've probably heard the adage "There's nothing wrong with talking to yourself. But when you start answering back, it's time to worry." Whoever came up with this quip was wrong. Talking aloud to yourself in public isn't a sign of positive mental health, but holding an internal dialogue is not only

normal, it's useful. Your inner conversations have a powerful impact on your emotional well-being. Becoming aware of
exactly what you are saying *to* yourself *about* yourself can help
you understand why you react the way you do to events and
people in your life. It can help you figure out who you are,
control your moods, repeat your successes, and short-circuit
your shortcomings.

The key, of course, is to uncover exactly what you are saying when you talk to yourself. The following is a quick self-talk
test that will help you zero in on your internal dialogue. Take
as much time as you need to honestly answer these ten questions, and, when you are finished, we'll help you identify your
self-talk style.

Self-Talk Test

1. You are hosting a dinner party, and everything goes pretty well
   except for dessert, when you realize you forgot to pick up the
   pastry shells for the ice cream. At the end of the evening you are
   most likely to say to yourself:

   A. Who cares? The evening was a great success.

   B. Sure, the dinner party went all right, but dessert was a
   failure.

   C. I ruined everything when I didn't remember to go to the
   bakery.

2. You have a project at work that requires your team's support, and you are very eager and excited to get moving on it. At a meeting, however, one of your colleagues raises numerous questions about your idea and suggests you hold off until the team has more time to think about it. You most likely say to yourself:

    A. He might have a good point.

    B. He doesn't trust me.

    C. He is either for me or against me.

3. The word that most aptly describes your internal dialogue about yourself is:

    A. Positive and upbeat

    B. Neutral and on the fence

    C. Negative and critical

4. You've just made a major mistake at work that potentially cost the company a major sale. You are most likely to say to yourself in the next day or two:

    A. I may have made a mistake, but I'm still a worthwhile person.

    B. I never measure up to the person I want to be.

    C. I'm worthless.

5. You enjoy a much-needed outing with friends. When you arrive home, you find your spouse sprawled on the couch watching

television, with leftover pizza and stacks of dirty plates and cups on the kitchen counter. You most likely say to yourself:

    A. My spouse must be exhausted. I'll whip those dishes into shape and then relax on the couch too.

    B. I never get to go out by myself. Couldn't my spouse at least be courteous enough to clean up this one time?

    C. I should never have gone out. Things completely fall apart when I'm gone.

6. When you were a kid, what kind of messages did you most often receive from your parents?

    A. Encouraging and loving messages

    B. An equal amount of encouraging and critical messages

    C. Critical and hurtful messages

7. You are headed out for the evening and want to wear one of your favorite shirts. It is just finishing the final cycle in your washing machine. You put it in the dryer and the dryer shorts out. It's completely dead—no power. And your shirt is completely wet. You realize it won't be dry in time to wear it. You most likely say to yourself:

    A. No problem, I'll wear something else.

    B. It never fails. This always happens to me.

    C. I can't stand this. My whole evening is ruined.

8. You are needing a helping hand to move some heavy furniture and wondering about asking a friend. What thought is most likely to shoot through your brain?

   A. I'm pretty sure he can help, and if not, he'll say so.

   B. Am I pushing the limits of this friendship too far?

   C. I don't deserve to have anyone help me, and I better not even ask.

9. Your tennis opponent says out loud to himself, "What a lousy shot!" You are most likely to:

   A. Say, "You're being too hard on yourself."

   B. Remain silent.

   C. Say, "You're right; I've seen better."

10. In general, the internal conversation you have with yourself most days tends to:

    A. Help you experience more fully and consistently your profound significance.

    B. Go back and forth between helping and hindering your experience of profound significance.

    C. Keep you from experiencing your profound significance.

Scoring

If you answered mainly "A," it's safe to say that your self-talk is based on a solid sense of significance. You tend to consistently see things in their proper perspective and rarely punish yourself for mistakes. Your self-talk is based on the reality of the situation. If your shirt was wet, for example, you simply chose another shirt. No big deal. Also, your negative situations don't tend to elicit a negative emotional response. This is a sure sign of well-schooled self-talk. Plus, if you've made a mistake, you don't see *yourself* as a mistake—a sure sign of profound significance. In general, you are secure in yourself and enjoy a depth of self-worth. You have learned to use your self-talk as a tool to maintain your dignity and significance. Of course, if nearly every one of your answers was in this category, you may want to review how honest you are being with yourself. Rarely does a person answer every item with an "A."

If you answered mainly "B," your self-talk tends to be more negative than is beneficial. While you are not likely to punish yourself for very long with a condemning internal dialogue, you certainly are not using your self-talk to maximize your experience of profound significance. You are literally talking yourself out of the full enjoyment of being loved at your core. There is much you can learn to improve your self-talk, and the remainder of this chapter will help you do just that.

If you answered mainly "C," your self-talk shows signs of needing serious attention and repair. Likely, you are suffering from a low sense of self-worth, and your self-talk is keeping at bay any chance of experiencing profound significance. Almost reflexively, you immediately equate any failure or bad experience to your own "badness." You have a very difficult time separating who you are from what you do. No doubt you already know your internal dialogue is repeatedly sabotaging your ability to receive your significance and worth. What can you do? Plenty. The remainder of this chapter is dedicated to helping you improve your self-talk. We will show you how you can begin to maximize it in numerous ways.

Are the results of a self-test like these generalizations? Of course. Since we aren't meeting with you one-on-one, face-to-face, we don't have the luxury of examining unique nuances and subtleties of how you use or abuse yourself through internal dialogue. However, this simple self-test can at least help you *identify* your general tendencies so you can get the most out of this chapter.

The Best Kind of Self-Talk

If you've ever read about Winston Churchill, you know that his self-talk played a huge role in helping him lead England through its most turbulent times. Although his life was racked by emotional neglect, parental hypocrisy, and excessive expectations, he kept saying the right things to himself. He kept believing in himself as a human being.

After slogging through failure after failure in his early education, Churchill's inner conversation eventually made a survivor of him. And this internal dialogue was best revealed in a commencement speech he made at Harrow School in 1941. Approaching the podium with his trademark cigar, cane, and top hat, he gave a speech that consisted of only six words— six words that had clearly cut a groove and worn a path in his brain. Gazing steadily at his waiting audience, Churchill finally shouted with the confidence of long experience, "Never give up!" Several seconds passed before he rose to his toes and shouted again, "Never give up!" Then he slowly reached for his top hat and his cigar, steadied himself with his cane, and left the platform. In those few words he had shared the most powerful advice he had to share—the personal self-talk that had carried him from mediocrity to the heights of leadership.

And those same words—"Never give up!"—can lift you up too.

But don't confuse positive self-talk with happy affirmations—or even worse, self-delusion. Let's say you can't carry a tune in a bucket. You simply don't have much musical ability with your voice. If you tell yourself that if you only try harder, you can learn to be a virtuoso, that self-talk would be positive but flawed. If you were to tell yourself that you're no good at singing, your self-talk would be negative but not flawed. On the other hand, if you were to say to yourself that you can't do anything right (because you can't sing), that would be flawed, overgeneralized thinking.

> This is my prayer: that your love may abound more and more in knowledge and depth of insight, so that you may be able to discern what is best and may be pure and blameless for the day of Christ.
>
> —PAUL, IN PHILIPPIANS 1:9–10 NIV

The best kind of self-talk is not self-hype or excessively positive. Nor is it negative, flawed, or overgeneralized. It is logical, rational, and accurate.

In a landmark study, Stanford University's Albert Bandura, internationally known for his work in personality, showed that while the clear majority of us spend lots of time worrying about things we can't control, healthy and successful people attend primarily to those things that are relevant and within their control.

Let's make this clear. The best kind of self-talk is rational. It says, *I choose my responses; they don't choose me.* It says, *No thought can dwell in my mind without my permission.* It says, *My value does not equal my performance.*

The Worst Kind of Self-Talk

Not long ago, while traveling through Memphis, we visited the Lorraine Motel. Standing in the small parking lot of the motel, it didn't take much to imagine what it must have been like that April day in 1968 when Martin Luther King Jr. stepped outside room 306 and was assassinated. We stood there solemnly and read a bit of information about the tragedy that made headlines around the world. As we read, we learned about another death associated with his murder that few have heard about. It was the wife of the owner of the motel where King was staying. On hearing the news of King's murder, the woman collapsed and died the next day.

Death from emotional shock is rare, but it underscores how lethal our internal thinking can be. Who knows

> Until you value yourself, you won't value your time. Until you value your time, you will not do anything with it.
>
> —M. SCOTT PECK

what self-talk this poor woman invented upon learning this news? What we do know is that some forms of self-talk are far more damaging than others. These are the statements that stem from our negative inner voice, our pathological critic.

Rhonda, a twenty-nine-year-old mother of two, let herself have it the other night. "I was looking forward to a hot shower after a hectic day, but as I was getting undressed, I knocked over a bathroom plant. There was dirt and pottery everywhere, and I found myself saying, 'Rhonda, why are you so clumsy?' I don't even speak to my children that way!"

Most often this vicious and vocal critic compares you to others—their achievements and abilities. It sets up impossible standards and then tears you down for not meeting them. It calls you names: stupid, incompetent, ugly, selfish, weak. Your negative inner voice tells you that your friends are bored, your spouse is annoyed, your parents are disappointed, your colleagues are disgusted. Your pathological critic, if not tamed, will undermine your dignity at every turn. And according to some experts, as much as 77 percent of the average person's self-talk is negative.

Consider this scenario. Your boss calls you into his office and asks you to present your vision for the company's new advertising campaign. "I've called a special meeting of the board of directors and I want them to hear from you and a couple other of our employees." At first you are flattered. Then you start thinking, *I'm terrible in front of groups. I stumble all over my words. I'll end up a fool.* Your face doesn't show it. Your boss only knows he has just given you an enviable assignment.

Or did he? *Maybe he wants to see me fail,* you begin to reason. *Maybe he wants the board to see what an idiot I am so he can fire me.* Walking back to your office, you snap out of it. *That's silly,* you say. *I'm overreacting—why do I do that? I'm so stupid.*

That night over dinner your spouse congratulates you on your opportunity, but you say to yourself, *She doesn't know the real me. I'm such a fraud.* You're up so late working on your remarks that you actually consider declining your boss's request. *But then he'd know I'm the loser I really am,* you tell yourself.

This steady stream of poison feels normal and true if you have given credence to such internal lies. Your pathological critic is incredibly toxic. Truly, it can be more poisonous to your psychological health than almost any trauma or loss. That's because grief and pain normally diminish over time, but the critic, if not curbed, is always with you—judging, blaming, and finding fault. *There you go again,* says the internal critic, *being an idiot.*

If you too often fall victim to your pathological critic, if it is eroding your self-worth, there is hope. We have a plan. We have a way to shut down your internal condemnation. But first you need to be able to identify your self-talk style.

How to Change Your Negative Self-Talk

You see them everywhere. Little inspirational sayings like, "You are the only one who can limit your greatness." Or, "Make your optimism come true." They are on posters in gyms and offices. Social media is plastered with them. Do they help? Do they work? Well, if you're feeling harried because of a stressful commute and a looming project, a kid with the sniffles, not to mention a pile of laundry sitting in a corner at home and a to-do list that stretches to the horizon, is a pithy platitude really going to turn things around for you? Maybe. If you don't feel guilty for not measuring up, a powerful quote might give you a boost. You may suddenly feel a surge of motivation. It can shape your self-talk in that moment to take positive action. But for a deeper and abiding change, you'll need more than a feel-good slogan. You'll need more than inspiration to change your ongoing internal dialogue.

> [The Christian] does not think God will love us because we are good, but that God will make us good because He loves us.
>
> —C. S. LEWIS

Inspiration has its place. But ultimately inspiration that comes from the outside is synthetic. It won't last for long. It has a short shelf life when it comes to deep, life-changing self-talk. It may be helpful, even necessary at times, but it's not enough. Don't be hoodwinked by the "inspirational-industrial complex." Long-lasting and life-transforming inspiration has to arise from a deeper place. True and lasting change is an inside job that has nothing to do with performance.

It doesn't matter if you're married or single, young or old, shy or assertive: if your self-worth hangs on a condition of good performance, your self-talk is sure to be riddled with self-doubt, insecurity, and anxiety. After the upbeat quotes become white noise, your inner voice is bound to be condemning. Why? Because, as French philosopher Blaise Pascal said, there is an "infinite abyss" in the heart of each of us that can be filled only by God. And until we fill that abyss with God's love—until we feel it deep in our beings—our sense of worth and significance becomes illusive. We will never be fully satisfied. We will never have a solid foundation of love to stand on. Healthy people plant their feet firmly on a deep and confident sense of worth that is built by God's love. They recognize that God created them and that he knows them intimately and loves them—no matter what. They think of themselves as "wonderfully made" (Ps. 139:14 NIV). They have *intrinsic* worth that no longer depends on performance.

We could give you a list of psychological tricks and techniques to change your negative self-talk. But we prefer to cut right to the heart of the matter. So at the risk of sounding trite, the key to changing your negative self-talk into the best kind of self-talk is to experience God's love deep down in your soul. We're not talking about "knowing" God's love—which comes as a result of a studied and reasoned, or academic, pursuit. You can know things you don't experience. For example, you can argue that the Bible says God loves the world (John 3:16), and you are part of the world, so you are loved by God. That's a mental exercise. Not an experience.

In the 1700s, Jonathan Edwards used a simple analogy: "There is a difference between having a rational judgment that honey is sweet and having a sense of its sweetness." You can know honey is sweet because someone tells you, but you don't really know its sweetness until you've tasted it.

We're talking about opening your heart and allowing the sweetness of God's love to be experienced. This is more about your heart than your head. It's what John Wesley was getting at in pondering God's love when he described his heart as being "strangely warmed." Pascal, who was a mathematician and scientist as well as a philosopher, said his heart was "directed into the love of God." It's a feeling at the center of our beings. It's beyond *knowing* with your head. In fact, it's beyond comprehension. How can you wrap your head around being loved by the Creator—so much so that you *feel* it?

When I (Les) was a graduate student in seminary, a professor asked a class of more than fifty students: "How many of you experience God's love?" He quickly added, "Don't raise your hands on impulse. Think about it and only raise your hand if you know the feeling of being loved by God." Out of this room of students preparing for ministry, how many hands went up? Fewer than a dozen. Those who didn't raise their hands gave answers like "I know I'm supposed to say that I have . . . I know the Bible says he loves me . . . but I don't feel it." Some even admitted that God felt cold, aloof, and demanding—not loving.

The professor wasn't surprised. It wasn't his first time to pose the question to a class of students. He followed it up with another: "How many of you have been conscious of God's love for you, personally, in the past week?" No hands went up this time. He waited a couple of beats and continued: "How many have been conscious of God's disapproval of you this week?" Hands shot up all around the room.

If you want to experience God's love, if you want to feel it deep in your spirit, you've got to admit that you are indeed inadequate—that you haven't and will not ever earn God's love. It's an impossibility. You can only receive it as a grace gift. When God tells us, "Seek the LORD and his strength; seek his presence continually" (1 Chron. 16:11 ESV), he is not merely making a suggestion. He designed us to live with him. That's where we find health, wholeness, and fulfillment. Jesus underscored this when he said, "I came that they may have life and have it abundantly" (John 10:10 ESV).

> One who has been touched by grace will no longer look on those who stray as "those evil people" or "those poor people who need our help." Nor must we search for signs of "loveworthiness." Grace teaches us that God loves because of who God is, not because of who we are.
>
> —PHILIP YANCEY

You may feel as though a million hurdles stand in your way to experiencing God's love—guilt, shame, blame, perfectionism, legalism, inadequacies, hurts (we'll get to these in the next chapter)—but be assured that nobody has or ever will *earn* the love of God. Each of us is undeserving. But when we open our hearts to receive it and continually walk with God to experience it, our internal dialogue forever changes.

Instead of a momentary inspiration to get you to your next accomplishment so you can feel better about yourself, you find yourself feeling profoundly significant in front of your Creator and have a lifetime of motivation to be exactly who you were designed to be.

The payoff? Insecure feelings are few and far between. Worry wanes. Peace reigns. Your relationships become rich and vital. You are less defensive, more caring, generous, and attractive for all the right reasons. The more you tune in to and master your self-talk, the more you embrace just how profoundly significant you are in the eyes of your Creator. You are becoming healthy and whole.

Moving Past Your Past

Don't try to saw sawdust.

—WILLARD KEEFE

T hat's not the way I remember it!" Lauren exclaimed heat-
edly to her sister, Josey. "How could you think that about
our father?"

Josey narrowed her eyes in anger. It was the first reunion she'd had with her two sisters since their parents' deaths
two years earlier. And this was why. Anytime she tried to talk
with Lauren and Annette about their father and the way he
had treated them, they could never see eye to eye. It was as
if her sisters had lived in a different home. As if they hadn't
experienced his cutting remarks (they called them his sense
of humor, his sarcasm, and said that's the way he related to

others) or been hurt by him constantly missing their concerts and games (they said it was because he had a strong work ethic and knew their family needed the money from his overtime whenever possible).

So who was right? Who had the truth? The sisters may never know because they all remember their homelife differently. But a kind friend who really cared about Josey finally shared with her what he saw: that she was using her anger against her father to keep her from becoming close to *any* man. Why? Because she was afraid of being hurt or feeling ignored again. That anger was poisoning her relationship with a man who loved her deeply and wanted to marry her. And it was also poisoning her relationship with her sisters, who longed to invite Josey more often into their homes.

Josey had to make a choice—to stay rooted in her anger against her father, or to let her bitterness go and move on past her past. The choice would not be easy, but it was one she knew she would have to make.

And Josey isn't the only one who has a choice to make. All of us are shaped by our memories—whether factual or interpretations. Our past can either help us become confident of our significance and our decisions or cause us to plod through life, uncertain of our worth, anxious about our present, and too paralyzed to make good decisions about our future.

If you do not correctly understand how your past—whether accurately recalled or simply imagined—is shaping your present, you will forever be stuck in it, never achieving the level of profound significance emotional health requires.

As you saw in the last chapter, your self-talk is key to re-inforcing the love that emanates from a caring God. But if you stop there, without learning to move past your past, you will forever be slowed down on your journey to wholeness. Your proverbial baggage is sure to weigh you down.

Why Dwelling on the Past Is Self-Defeating

Dwelling on the past is like driving your car with your foot on the brake, your eyes on the rearview mirror, and your gas tank empty. You're wondering why you aren't moving forward, and yet all the while you're focused on the wrong direction. Even if you want to make progress, dwelling on your past keeps you stuck and prevents you from embracing your profound significance.

> The past beats inside me like a second heart.
>
> —JOHN BANVILLE

For example, let's say you want to lose weight. But instead of being proactive—checking out exercise and diet programs—you blame your mother for "conditioning" you to clean your plate at every meal. Whether your mother did this or not isn't the real issue. The real issue is what you're going to do about it now. If you don't take steps to lose weight, you never will.

You may want to save money, but if your excuse is never having a father who modeled financial savvy (whether he did or not), you'll live from paycheck to paycheck.

You may want to be more intentional about dating and finding a potential spouse, but if you say you're shy because you were raised this way (whether you were or not), you'll probably stay home again this Friday night.

No matter how much you'd like to change, if you are blaming your real or imagined past for your present, you're not going anywhere. You'll be permanently stuck in your rut. Sitting in the same place may be "comfortable" because you don't have to take a risk, but is that really the way you want to live your life?

Let's make this perfectly clear: Bad things happen in this world. Sometimes they are of your own choosing—because you made a poor decision. Other times bad things happen because there is evil in the world and even the saintliest among us are not promised an easy ride. Bad things happen to good people.

However, we want you to know that regret, blame, and excuses are a dead end. When your focus is on the lack of nurture your parents provided you as a child, or a mistake you made three years ago that plunged your finances into the red, or the devastating embarrassment your sister caused you as a teenager, or an opportunity you passed up six months ago to initiate a date with an attractive person, then you have a "good" excuse for giving up. After all, if you didn't get the lucky breaks or privileges others did, or you didn't receive the treatment you thought you deserved, or you were dealt a hand that could barely be played, or you made a choice that was clearly dim-witted, your situation is hopeless. Deep down, when you excavate your way through the layers of excuses, accusations, and blame, you could really be asking a simple question: *Why try? It won't make any difference anyway.*

Truth be told, we know that's exactly what you're saying whenever you choose to be stuck in the past—because research has clearly revealed it. Every time you make an excuse for failing in the present, every time you cast your gaze to the past for an explanation of your current predicament, you are convincing yourself that your problem is more and more hopeless. In fact—and this is key—your excuses are producing the very kind of problem behavior you are attempting to explain.

> Yesterday is but today's memory and tomorrow is today's dream.
>
> —KAHLIL GIBRAN

Let's take Dave for an example. For years he's blamed his problems in relationships on his overbearing mother and his distant father. *I just can't get anybody to like me*, he tells himself—and he acts on that. Although he's physically attractive and has garnered many dates as a result, he booby-traps every date by showing up late, forgetting his wallet, or talking only about himself. *My parents just never taught me to relate to others*, he insists. Well, perhaps they did—and perhaps they didn't. But again, that isn't the issue. Because Dave thinks he can't relate to others, he isn't even trying—and as a result, he doesn't relate well to others.

At the University of Kansas, C. R. Snyder and Raymond L. Higgins have studied the excuses people make for irresponsible, self-defeating behavior. What they have found may surprise you.

First, excuses soften the link between you and an unfortunate action. That's the seduction of a good excuse. *I can't control my anger because I've always been this way. I'll never find my soul mate because I seem to only attract the neediest. I'll be in debt forever because my family could never save money.* All these excuses and millions more put a distance between you and your failures. They provide a modicum of comfort because you can explain your angry outbursts, your failed relationships, your financial woes by pointing to something beyond yourself.

And that's why, for the short-term, we all need excuses. They protect our dignity and keep a fragile sense of self-esteem from crumbling. But these same excuses, when they linger too long, become our rationalizations for staying stuck.

Dwelling on the past—whether real or imagined—is a road that will never lead to personal growth and health of mind. In fact, it clearly prevents it. You may never know, on this earth, if what you remember happening to you is the truth or not. But you do have a choice now—to decide whether you will continue dragging around any past baggage or to remain stuck in a "poor me" victim mentality. Don't define yourself by your past. Don't allow yourself to continue as a helpless slave to a problem. If you do, you will never actively take charge of your life. Instead, you will continually hand over control of the problem—and, thus, your future life—to others.

Exploring Your Emotional Baggage

Ever thought about what's in the luggage that makes the rounds at the baggage claim area in the airport? As you are waiting for your own bags to arrive, perhaps you think to yourself or say to a friend, "That monogrammed Louis Vuitton piece must surely contain valuables. That hot-pink Samsonite number with the stickers on it looks intriguing. Wonder who owns that cardboard box held together with duct tape and string. Or how about that sleek silver case with the sturdy lock?"

Allow us to ask what may seem like a strange or even silly question: If your psychological baggage were traveling on that same conveyor belt at the airport, what kind of shape would it be in? How would it look? Would it be scuffed up? Tightly locked? Nondescript? How would you describe it?

We ask because your answer reveals a bit about how you

> The past is a foreign country; they do things differently there.
>
> —L. P. HARTLEY

consider your past. It provides a glimpse into your feelings about your personal history. And those feelings are what we psychologists are getting at when we talk about your proverbial baggage.

History is what has happened in our lives. *Baggage* is how we feel about it. And we all have baggage. Even the most well-adjusted and healthiest people have baggage. No one is exempt. You may have childhood angst over parental divorce, conflicts with friends and family, or remorse over missteps and lost opportunities. Everyone has a history and an emotional response to it. What matters, when it comes to being a healthy human being, is whether you have deliberately unpacked your baggage. If not, it is bound to thwart your personal growth. You can never feel profoundly significant at your core until you make peace with this emotional baggage. The healthiest among us, you can be sure, have rummaged around in the contents of their own suitcases. They have explored what they feel and why they feel the way they do about their history. And this act of simply identifying and labeling their emotions as they explore their past serves as an amazing springboard to personal growth, self-insight, and maturity. It even affects physical well-being.

> Go forth to meet the shadowy Future, without fear.
>
> —HENRY WADSWORTH LONGFELLOW

Consider the following study, which is only one among

hundreds that substantiate this point. Participants were asked to write for just fifteen minutes a day about a disturbing experience. They did this for three or four days in a row. Forget polish and politeness. The point was not to craft a wonderful essay but to dig deeply into one's emotional junkyard, then translate the experience onto the page. James Pennebaker, a psychology professor at the University of Texas at Austin and author of the study, then compared a group of college students who wrote about trauma with a group who wrote about trivial things (how they named their pet or the kinds of clothes they like). Before the study, the forty-six students in the study had visited the campus health clinic at similar rates. But after the exercise, the trauma writers' visits dropped by 50 percent relative to the others. Other studies have found that identifying one's feelings about past events increases the level of disease-fighting lymphocytes circulating in the bloodstream. It also lowers blood pressure.

Notice an important distinction. Spending time with your past, coming to terms with it, putting it in perspective, is different from wallowing in your past and using it as a scapegoat. In order to get *beyond* your past, you sometimes need to get *into* your past.

At this point you may be shaking your head. *No way am I going to relive that. Especially when I'll get hurt all over again—and it won't change a thing!*

You're right—reliving your past may hurt. And that's not fun. But you're also wrong; spending time with your past does change things. In fact, it can change your entire life perspective. So hang in there with the process. Coming to terms with your past isn't easy, but it's necessary for you to move on—to not only like your current life but love your current life and have great hope for the future. The very process of exploring, identifying, and owning your emotional response to your history is what will allow you to move past your past. Contrary to what many of us may think, healthy people are not blessed with an unblemished history. Rather, they suffer the same struggles as you do. But they carry their negative history with little ill effect because they understand it to be part of their story. They have come to grips with the hurtful emotions a family member engenders, for example, and they acknowledge when those emotions arise.

Because they have traced back the source of their hurt, examined it from different angles, they are able to set it aside. Their emotional baggage no longer pulls them down. In fact, they may even learn to joke about it in a healthy way. (Think about it: one person's dysfunctional family background is another's entertaining tale or comedy routine.)

> Who controls the past controls the future: who controls the present controls the past.
>
> —GEORGE ORWELL

If you want to become the person you were meant to be, you've got to unpack your baggage. Here's our step-by-step plan for doing just that.

How to Move Past Your Past

Before we write another word, we want to be clear and up-front: If you do what we are about to suggest, it doesn't mean you will never struggle with your past again. Nope. That's a fool's errand. This is not a "miracle cure" for overcoming every negative effect from your past. But these three practical steps—or more accurately challenges—have proven immeasurably helpful to countless people. If you take on these three challenges, you are sure to gain better control over your past and reach a higher level of emotional health.

1. Identify Your Emotional Triggers

Judy says her divorce has long been put to rest. After all, it has been nearly twenty years. But whenever Judy hears Ken's name, she immediately remembers that he bitterly betrayed her, and she still feels that old anger rise up within her. Twenty years after the fact, Judy is allowing the baggage of her divorce to determine her emotional state. Why? Because she has never put her finger on exactly what triggers her anger. She has never owned the fact that she still wants Ken to pay a painful price for what he put her through. "He deserves at least as much hurt as I have experienced," she confides to her counselor. "Ken turned his back on me and our two children and he deserves to suffer for that."

Maybe so. But guess who has been suffering more for two decades—Ken or Judy? There's no contest. Judy has been carrying this emotional baggage so long she has forgotten that there is any other way. She has stayed stuck, hung up on her divorce, because she continues to focus her thinking on what Ken did to her. She has every right to be angry. To be hurt. But that's not the issue. If she wants to change, if she wants to get unstuck and move forward, she's got to pinpoint what's really happening. She's got to own up to the unfinished business of her divorce. If she doesn't, it will forever rule her emotions.

> I always get to where I am going by walking away from where I have been.
>
> —WINNIE THE POOH

If you can identify something in your past that is complicating your existence, similar to Judy's scenario, we have a challenge. Grab something to write with and answer these questions:

- What relationships or experiences from my past still stir up negative emotions?
- What strong negative emotions do I feel? Label the emotions one by one and write them down.
- What does my "self-talk" say about this relationship or experience? In other words, how am I interpreting this memory?

Don't put this off. Take time to do it now if you can. It will help you begin to pinpoint your thinking.

2. Shake Off Excuses

Before we even start to talk about this next step, we want you to try "The Excuse Finder." It's a simple fill-in-the-blank exercise.

One of the most popular self-help moments of recent years has focused on a deterministic perspective that revolves around the "inner child." This theory says that the traumas of childhood—rather than our own decisions or our character— have caused the problems we are experiencing today as adults. The purported cure, in this line of thinking, is to overcome our "victimization" by delving into these early traumas, some-times reexperiencing them, with an inner-child guru who will help us scream through the pain or imagine different outcomes.

We take a different point of view. Maybe you were trauma-tized as a child. Maybe you were mistreated and emotionally harmed. If so, you have reason to be angry and resentful. Every child deserves better. And that never should have happened to you. But all the wishing in the world cannot change the facts: you have baggage as a result.

However, if your bad childhood events have become the hook upon which to hang your adult problems, you're not going to be able to move forward in life. You won't become that healthy, happy, significant self you long to be. Nor will you have lasting, satisfying relationships.

It all comes down to choice. Your choice. Just because you've had a difficult personal history doesn't mandate that you must be a troubled adult. Consider the research.

You might expect to find massive evidence for the destructive effect of neglect, beatings, parental death or divorce, physical illness, and sexual abuse on the adulthood of the victims. But large-scale, costly surveys of adult mental health, for the most part, have revealed something different: People who have suffered terrible things are not predestined to live in misery. Some do, of course. But stories abound of those who have made a different choice—a choice to rise above injustice and pain.

There are countless stories of people who have risen above their tough circumstances. Oprah Winfrey is a classic example. She was repeatedly molested by her cousin, uncle, and a family friend. She gave birth at age fourteen to a baby who soon died. But her success today is known around the globe. Actress Charlize Theron, at fifteen, witnessed her mother kill her father. Instead of letting the trauma immobilize her, she channeled her energy into acting and eventually won an Academy Award. Richard Branson, the British business mogul, grew up with dyslexia and failed repeatedly in school. Bethany Hamilton, a competitive surfer, was just thirteen when an almost-deadly shark attack resulted in her losing her left arm. Two years later, she won first place in the national surfing championship. Actor Jim Carrey had to drop out of school to

> What you leave behind says as much about you as what you bring along.
>
> —JACQUELYN MIDDLETON

support his family while they were living in a van. The list goes on and on: Nelson Mandela, Helen Keller, Winston Churchill, Rosa Parks, Marie Curie, J. K. Rowling, Jesse Owens, and Malala Yousafzai. All these notable people overcame incredible challenges that could have understandably caused them to get stuck and quit trying.

Studies do not justify blaming whatever you're struggling with today—depression, anxiety, a bad marriage, drug use, sexual problems, unemployment, anger—on what happened to you years ago. The pain from your past is overrated. If you sincerely want to move past the pain and anger your past engenders, you can no longer lean on it to explain your current problems, whatever they are. You've got to shake off excuses, take responsibility for your current choices, and embrace the freedom you now have to make new ones.

If you're serious about shaking off your excuses, here's another challenge. Complete these sentence stems (really—write them down).

- If I didn't suffer from (whatever painful thing in your past) . . .
- I'm a victim of my circumstances because . . .
- The person in my past whom I'm thinking of doesn't deserve forgiveness because . . .
- The struggles I have today wouldn't exist if . . .

Okay. Did you do it? Or did you just read over these sentence stems without writing down your answers? Don't do that. Force

> All men make mistakes, but a good man yields when he knows his course is wrong, and repairs the evil. The only crime is pride.
>
> —SOPHOCLES

yourself to write even if this isn't easy. We want you to actually write them down. You won't need to share this with anyone. This is just for you. And if you take it seriously, it will help you detect where you are laying the blame for any of your challenges—and ultimately help you shake them off.

3. Excavate Your Feelings.

This third challenge is so simple, yet so powerful. Ready? Write about your feelings. You can use a pad of paper or your keyboard. If you're rolling your eyes at this idea, hang in there with us. We'll explain why and how this works in just a moment. But first the specific challenge:

- Reread your emotional triggers from the first challenge and choose one relationship or experience that still causes you emotional pain.
- For the next twenty minutes or so write intensively about your feelings. Don't worry about grammar. Nobody will see this but you. Write whatever comes out. For some people, their feelings come in a list. Others write disjointed sentences. But don't stop—write until you've put down as much of your pain, regret, loss, and grief as you possibly can.

If you follow through on this "Write Your Feelings" exercise—a tool used by countless professional therapists—you are almost certain to gain a sense of empowerment and freedom from your past. On many occasions we have heard a grateful client say, "Doc, the writing changed my life."

How can writing accomplish this? Research suggests that it's far more therapeutic than anyone ever knew. Since the mid-1980s, studies have found that people who write about their most upsetting experiences are more emotionally balanced, more confident, and less worried.

This exercise isn't a simple catharsis. It's more than that. Putting your emotions on paper transforms the ruminations cluttering your mind into coherent stories. Writing your feelings also dulls their impact. How is this possible? Because you are now articulating what used to lurk in murky emotional waters. You are uncovering what has been beneath so many of your emotional experiences.

> Realize that if you have time to whine and complain about something then you have the time to do something about it.
>
> —ANTHONY J. D'ANGELO

If you really want to see the benefits of this, write intensely for twenty minutes about your emotions two or three times during the next week. We know it's a simple idea, but it's time-tested and proven to work.

Summarizing a University of Michigan research project

on well-being, the researchers said that "having a strong sense of controlling one's life is a more dependable predictor of positive feelings of well-being than any of the objective conditions of life we have considered." In other words, after all the research on personal fulfillment is reviewed and tabulated, moving beyond the deadweight of your past and gaining control over your future is turning out to be one of the single most powerful predictors of positive mental health we have.

It's clear that to be healthy, to be content, to be fulfilled, to realize the truth about your inner significance, you must tune in to your self-talk and move past your past (John 8:32).

PART TWO

Unswerving
Authenticity

*What will it profit a man if he gains the
whole world, and loses his own soul?*

—JESUS, IN MARK 8:36 NKJV

I ask him that with both feet planted firmly on love, you'll be able to take in with all followers of Jesus the extravagant dimensions of Christ's love. Reach out and experience the breadth! Test its length! Plumb the depths! Rise to the heights! Live full lives, full in the fullness of God. . . .

I want you to get out there and walk—better yet, run!—on the road God called you to travel. I don't want any of you sitting around on your hands. I don't want anyone strolling off, down some path that goes nowhere. . . .

Pouring yourselves out for each other in acts of love, alert at noticing differences and quick at mending fences.

Ephesians 3:14–19; 4:1–3

R eal isn't how you were made. It's a thing that happens to you," said the toy horse. "When a child loves you for a long, long time, not just to play with, but really loves you, then you become Real."

This old toy horse in Margery Williams's classic children's story *The Velveteen Rabbit* not only squarely identifies the second essential step to health and wholeness, but wisely notes that it is the result of being loved.

Profound significance—which we've just explored in the past two chapters—is the precursor to unswerving authenticity. Without the foundation of knowing we are unconditionally loved, we cannot risk being authentic or real. But once we claim our significance and recognize its durability over time, we cultivate the rich soil of the soul for authenticity to take root.

What is *authenticity*? It's what separates the genuinely loving person from the person who merely wants to be *seen* as loving. It makes no room for imitation or fakery. No space for "phoning it in." There's no going through the motions. Authenticity divides those who walk the walk from those who merely talk it. When you are real, your head and heart work in harmony. You are the same person behind the curtain as you were onstage. You no longer perform to win love—that was settled when you embraced your significance. No. You've dismissed the audience from your life and tossed the script. Instead, who you are determines what you do. You are genuine.

Authenticity is all about *being* rather than *doing*. When

you focus on being genuinely loving, for example, the actions naturally follow. They are not contrived. There's no pretense. You don't wonder what you should do. Your doing flows naturally from your being. Health and wholeness mature at a remarkable rate as this important process unfolds.

And vulnerability is key to unswerving authenticity. Consider this statement: "You're the first person I have ever been completely honest with." Every psychologist has heard this sentence hundreds of times. But it was Sidney Jourard who made sense of them in his in-depth book *The Transparent Self.* He was puzzled over the frequency with which patients were more honest and authentic with a clinician than they were with family or friends. After much study, he concluded that each of us has a natural, built-in desire to be known, but we often stifle our vulnerability with the significant people in our lives out of fear. We're afraid of being seen as too emotional or not emotional enough, as too assertive or not assertive enough. We're afraid of rejection.

The result? We wear masks. We put up our guard. In Margery Williams's story, the toy rabbit didn't know real rabbits existed. He thought they were all stuffed with sawdust like himself. "And he understood that sawdust was quite out-of-date and should never be mentioned in modern circles." The rabbit kept authenticity at bay through his fear of being found out. He never wanted to risk vulnerability.

But we are never authentic until we admit our frustrations, acknowledge our weaknesses, and disclose our insecurities. We are never real until we open our wounded hearts. Everyone's

heart has been wounded. But most people would rather protect their wounds than divulge them. Healthy people, however,
make personal wounds available to others when needed.

No one has written more sensitively on the gift of vulnerability than Henri Nouwen in his book *The Wounded Healer*.
He points out that "making one's own wounds a source of
healing . . . does not call for a sharing of superficial personal
pains but for a constant willingness to see one's own pain and
suffering as rising from the depth of the human condition."

The point is that healthy, authentic people do not pretend
to have it all together. They do not present themselves as something they are not. They are honest about their imperfections,
problems, inadequacies, and pain. They do not relegate their
dark side to the basement of their personality. They do not try
to disown their failings or ignore their weaknesses. Instead,
they use them to propel themselves forward.

Think of it this way. If four people had to push a car in
need of gas across a street, what would be the best way for them
to push? Obviously, all four of them pushing together in the
same direction would maximize their likelihood of reaching
the common goal. When they align their efforts, they multiply
their power and optimize their efficiency.

Now imagine that this car represents your personality.
And what you think, feel, say, and do are the four people trying
to get the car across the street. For you to reach your highest
goals, these four separate parts of you must work in alignment,
all headed in the same direction. *Together.*

Being who you really are means lowering your defenses.

It may even mean a few acts of daring vulnerability now and then. It's the only way to grow. If you are pushing and pulling in all sorts of directions, not at all in alignment within yourself, your progress will be painfully slow. But if you find your way to inner harmony, if you get real, you will begin to move on a sure and steady course to a deeply meaningful and satisfying life.

Abraham Maslow called this—the working together of the separate parts of you—*congruency*. He considered it a major requirement for attaining the top level of his hierarchy of needs: fulfillment. We experience the peak of fulfillment when we become congruent. When we are *all of a piece*. Our thoughts, feelings, words, and actions are in sync. All the parts of us are striving together to help us reach our potential.

In every moment, then, our focus remains fixed on being the person we truly are. This unflinching determination to be authentic may lose us some friends or cost us some memberships or jobs, but the gains of being true to ourselves far outweigh the cost.

While everyone seems to have a plan for what we should do, the healthy person knows their purpose—the road God called them to follow. They stay on that road. Paul was so enthusiastic about unswerving authenticity in following this path that he urged us to not only walk but *run* on the path God calls us to travel (Eph. 4:1). This means we need to recognize what that path is and be authentically true to following that call—despite what others might think or say. No more suffering from the "disease to please." Instead, we are unswervingly authentic. How do we do this? Two actions: (1) we must uncover our blind spots to clearly see what God is showing us, and (2) we must face whatever fears are preventing us from following God's call.

When you get a lock on your profound significance and become more unswervingly authentic, emotional well-being takes a quantum leap. You rely on an internal gyroscope that keeps your bearings steady instead of tiptoeing around, guessing what you think others want you to be.

THREE

Uncovering Your
Blind Spots

There are [things] such as a man is afraid to reveal
even to himself, and every decent man will have
accumulated quite a few things of this sort.

—FYODOR DOSTOYEVSKY

Research shows that we don't know ourselves as well as we think we do. Psychological blind spots keep us from seeing the truth. They distort our perceptions. They trick us into believing in a reality that may not be true. And they feed us misinformation. Like the physical blind spots in automobiles, our personal blind spots steer us into danger if we're not careful.

Take thirty-year-old Michael, for instance, who complained to a friend that his wife didn't ever want him to go out with "the boys" or have any fun. In reality, Michael was out with his friends at least two nights a week. With their three young children at home, his wife was simply asking him to limit his nights with the boys to *one* night a week, so he could spend more time with the children.

It took a wise friend who had grown up with Michael to ask a question that finally opened his eyes: "Do you think you might be reacting to your wife as if she were your mother? Remember how your mom kept such tight control on you as a teenager that she barely let you go out on a Friday night?" Michael was stunned. He'd never considered the connection. Truly, this was a blind spot. But when Michael took off the blinders of anger and defensiveness, he realized *exactly* what was going on. He *was* penalizing his wife for the feelings he harbored against his mother.

Because of this realization, Michael was able to talk with his wife, apologize for his defensiveness, explain how he felt, and come up with a solution that worked well for the entire family: Michael still went out with the boys one night a week, but they also had a "Daddy" night each week when he focused on no one but the kids.

When the blinders come off, we see the truth. A new reality

> There are two ways to be fooled. One is to believe what isn't true; the other is to refuse to believe what is true.
>
> —SØREN KIERKEGAARD

sets in, just as it did for Michael. A transforming truth about who we are and how we are responding materializes where before we saw only an illusion. This is why discovering your blind spots is so crucial to getting and staying psychologically healthy. It's not easy work, but the payoffs are certainly sweet. It heightens your self-awareness, as we'll soon see in more detail, lowers your stress, revolutionizes your relationships, and frees your spirit for optimal fulfillment.

In short, self-awareness is curative. It uncovers your blind spots, allowing you to see who you really are.

Dr. Steven Pinker, a professor of psychology at Harvard University and author of ten books including *How the Mind Works*, says that self-awareness helps us maximize who we are. "Knowing thyself is a way of making thyself as palatable as possible to others."

Healthy people know themselves well. They know their strengths and limits, their likes and dislikes. They know what ticks them off and what soothes their spirit. They know their dark side and how to combat it. They monitor their feelings and learn how to manage them. They are aware of their motivations. They are aware of how they come off to others. Healthy people know, for the most part, what other people know about them. They work to keep their blind spots to a minimum.

Does this mean that awareness guarantees psychological health? No. But psychological health is impossible without knowing who you are. If you are in denial, you see yourself without any flaws and exaggerate your own abilities. You also dodge feedback at all cost. But if you are self-aware, you know the benefit of continuous critique. You know you can always improve by being more conscious—more alert to your emotions, your motives, your thinking, and your behavior.

The Unexamined Life

The Greek philosopher Plato recounts a trademark sound bite spoken by his pupil Socrates: "The unexamined life is not worth living." This ancient adage has extolled the virtues of self-exploration and heightened self-awareness for centuries. You'd think by now we humans would have it down. But we don't. Every generation of individuals must learn to examine their lives, to make their unconscious more conscious, and to diminish their blind spots to become unswervingly authentic. Why? Because we have a way of missing what's right in front of our noses.

We may think we know ourselves well, but all of us, to some degree, are oblivious to things that others easily see in us. And most likely we don't see these obvious aspects of who we are by our own design. We forget to recognize them in ourselves and then we forget that we've forgotten. In other words, we unconsciously deny ourselves access to certain aspects of our personality because we wish they weren't there. We reflexively avoid them because they cause fear, anxiety, or pain.

Is becoming unswervingly authentic always easy and pain-free? No. In fact, the anxiety of coming to terms with who we really are caused comedian Lily Tomlin to quip, "Reality is the leading cause of stress among those in touch with it." Getting in touch with the real you can cause stress. We are the first to admit it. Realizing who you really are may not be fun—but it is the only way to become the person you'd like to be. It's the only way to enjoy emotional and fulfilling relationships.

> Become aware of internal experiences so that it immediately becomes possible for a certain amount of control to be exerted over these hither unconscious and uncontrollable processes.
>
> —ABRAHAM HAROLD MASLOW

We all share a tendency toward denial. We filter out information, rationalize mistakes, avoid responsibility. Many of us will do just about anything to steer clear of the truth if it might hurt. Because—let's be honest—who *wants* to be hurt? To make the matter worse, the people around us—whether a close friend, spouse, boss, or coworker—may avoid honest, constructive feedback because they fear hurting or angering us.

If we are not intentional about self-awareness, we buy the illusion of harmony at the cost of the truth. And we miss the path that could take us to emotional maturity and psychological health.

Three Common Blind Spots

Have you ever been surprised by someone's description of you? Maybe they said you were outgoing when you thought of yourself as shy. Or perhaps they said you were insensitive when you thought you were compassionate. When a surprising description emerges, it almost always gives you pause. It may also give you a glimpse into an aspect of yourself you've never acknowledged.

For example, you may think of yourself as hardworking, but others may see you as hard-driving. You may think of yourself as straightforward and honest, but others may see you as self-righteous. You may think you handle your money well, but others may call you a tightwad. You may think you handle criticism well, but your body language tells others you are defensive. You may think you are aggressive and productive at work, but coworkers may see in you an insatiable need for recognition. You may think you're just staying in shape and "improving your looks," but your friends are convinced you are obsessed with your appearance, and they worry about your health.

And these are just a few examples. The list of potential blind spots seems endless. But some areas that are most commonly pushed out of our awareness deserve to be highlighted. And that's exactly what we want to do next—take a glimpse at the three most common blind spots to see if any are blinding you.

We Are Blind to Our Dark Side

The best people, the healthiest, are not exempt from miserable parts. Everyone has tendencies toward meanness, selfishness, envy, materialism, cruelty, dishonesty, lust, and irresponsibility. In fact, the more of these miserable parts we have, the stronger our potential for greatness. Why? Because your character is hammered out not in the *absence* of negative traits but *because* of them. Your struggle to overcome selfishness, for example, will make your generous spirit, once honed, far more prized, meaningful, and valuable than if it had come more easily or more naturally to you.

> Oh, would [God]
> the gift us
> to see ourselves
> as others see us!
>
> —ROBERT BURNS

We've seen many well-intentioned religious people work diligently to block out or bury their baser parts. They operate under the false assumption that if they ignore such bad tendencies, their dark side will disappear. Healthy people take a different approach. They come to terms with the rotten parts of their nature, eventually learn why they have them, and most important, they learn how to subdue, control, and even transform them. At the end of this chapter, we'll give you proven strategies for doing just that.

Meanwhile, steel your courage and risk delving into your own "dark side" by pondering these questions:

- What part of yourself are you most ashamed of, and how do you hide it from yourself and others?
- What "personality traits" or emotions tend to

repeatedly get you in trouble (such as pride, anger, jealousy, anxiety)?

- On a scale of one to ten, how motivated are you to learn better ways of coping with your dark side? Why?

We Are Blind to Our Limits

We've done enough marriage counseling with couples to know that the "presenting problem" is often not the problem at all. Every couple has deficits. But struggling couples typically don't know what theirs are. "We just don't know how to communicate," they might say. In a sense, this may be true, but their real deficit is that they don't know how to make time for meaning- ful communication, or they may have kept their feelings boxed up, or any number of things. Communication breakdowns are only a symptom of their real problem. And if they weren't blind to this fact, they could work on the real problem which would, by default, improve their communication problem.

> Most of us do not monitor our thoughts with the care needed so that we can create in our lives the results we say we want.
>
> —SIDNEY MADWED

The same holds true in work settings. In a comparison of executives who floundered and those who succeeded, both groups had weaknesses; the critical difference was that those who did not succeed failed to learn from their mistakes and accurately assess and accept their shortcomings. The unsuccessful executives ignored their faults, often rebuffing those who tried to point them out. Among several hundred managers from twelve different organizations, "accuracy in self-assessment was a hallmark of superior performance," according to author Daniel Goleman. It's not that top performers have no limits, he says, but "they are *aware* of their limits."

We Are Blind to Our Egoism

You have just returned from an amazing vacation to the Galápagos Islands, but after the obligatory "How was your trip?" the conversation with a friend turns to and remains on them. They tell you about a deadline they are under at work, a conversation with their spouse, or a movie they just saw. They seem oblivious to you and your recent experience—and they are. How does this happen? Egoism.

Welcome to the world of the oblivious egotist who, if reading these words, would have a very difficult time acknowledging that they are this person. But we still must ask: Is there any possibility this might describe you?

Peer evaluations are commonplace in universities. And after reviewing countless performance appraisals as professors, we have seen a phenomenon we've now come to expect. Some people simply cannot imagine that they are not as good as they think they are.

Here's a quick way to measure your egoism: Think about the last conversation you had before you read this. Then ask yourself, *Did I focus on myself—or the other person?* Better yet, review several recent conversations with the same question. The answer will tell you how much leaning toward egoism you might have.

The High Price of the Unexamined Life

The creators of the *Titanic* spared no expense to make sure it would be unsinkable. The ship's officers were unconcerned by their inability to get accurate information on possible hazards that might lie in its course. The ship had two lookouts on her masts, but the lookouts had no binoculars. In fact, they didn't even know about a potential iceberg. And even if they had known, the binoculars had been accidently locked inside a locker, and due to a mix-up there was no key. Many experts now suggest that binoculars would not have helped as it was a moonless night, and the sea was glassy calm, thus masking the line between the true and false horizons and camouflaging the iceberg. In addition, recent meteorological research suggests there was a mirage on the horizon that night created by cold water meeting warm air (like a water mirage in the

> The greatest of faults . . . is to be conscious of none.
>
> —THOMAS CARLYLE

desert), which would have resulted in an extraordinary bending of light, blinding the lookouts from spotting anything far away. In any case, the lookouts didn't see the iceberg until it was too late.

We all know what happened. The unsinkable ocean liner went to her death, along with most of her passengers, on her maiden voyage from Europe to New York: the victim of a disastrous collision with an iceberg.

What you don't see *can* hurt you. For example, you can convince yourself that if you submerge the dark side of your personality, ignoring its presence, it won't bother you. But you're wrong. Dead wrong. What you bury has a high rate of resurrection. Somehow, somewhere, it will pop up through the surface and be uglier than when you first buried it.

Let's say you abhor envy and petty jealousy in others. It's the last thing you would like to find in yourself, so you literally turn a blind eye. You act as if envy would never *ever* take up residence in you. But it has. It may not live on the main floor, but like the rest of your dark side, it is locked away in the basement. Left alone long enough, unchecked, envy grows. And when you least expect it—maybe when your child has a great success, or your friend gets a huge promotion—it bursts through the basement door of your personality and wreaks havoc throughout your whole house, fracturing the relationships you prize the most.

Sometimes the price we pay for our blind spots is not seen in an abrupt eruption, but it is paid more slowly over time. Say you are blind to your egoism. You may be charismatic and likeable, but you haven't a clue how to really enter another person's world—and you don't know it. The emotional capability to walk in someone else's shoes, to imagine what their experience must be like, is foreign to you. But the people in your life put up with this "quirk." They don't expect you to invest emotionally in them. Your enthusiasm or your business savvy or your humor make up for this interpersonal deficiency. People may come to respect you and your talent, but, sadly, they may not like you.

Let's make this plain. The price you pay for too many blind spots is a distortion of reality. You trade the truth for a false sense of security. By avoiding the facts of a negative trait you possess, you numb yourself to critics who point it out. In the short-term your blind spots guard against the incumbent anxiety and pain that accepting the truth might bring. But this tactic comes with a high price: skewed perceptions and a warped personality. It is no exaggeration to say that your blind spots, if unchecked, may eventually cost you a friendship, a job, a marriage, and, most certainly, your peace of mind.

Three Payoffs for Increasing Self-Awareness

As we've seen, it's easy to go blind to troubling or frightening information about ourselves. But when we gain our self-insight, we are rewarded well in at least three areas.

1. Self-Awareness Lowers Stress

An experiment requiring people to watch a graphic anti-drunk-driving film depicting bloody automobile accidents lends credence. In the half hour after viewing the film, many subjects reported feelings of tension, distress, and depression. They found themselves repeatedly thinking of upsetting scenes they had just witnessed. Those viewers who were aware of their emotions, who could identify more precisely what their experience was, however, recovered from their feelings of distress far more quickly.

Another study focused on people who were laid off. Many were, understandably, angry. Half were told to keep a journal for five days, spending twenty minutes writing out their deepest feelings (a common exercise in raising self-awareness). Those who kept journals found new jobs faster than those who didn't. Their heightened self-awareness lowered stress and more quickly enabled productivity.

> An anxious heart weighs a man down.
> —PROVERBS 12:25

Emotional clarity enables you to manage bad moods. It soothes your frustrations, calms your annoyances. In short, self-awareness lowers your stress. Richard Lazarus, in his book *Emotion and Adaptation*, reported on a college professor who was given a portable heart-rate monitor to wear because of his heart problems. Doctors feared that little oxygen was reaching the professor's heart muscle, but they needed to accurately assess how his heart was beating throughout a typical day. On this day the professor attended one of his regular and far-too-frequent departmental meetings—something he considered a waste of time.

But this typical day revealed something the professor was surprised to find—something he was completely unaware of. He learned from the monitor that, while he thought he was cynically detached from the discussions, his heart was pounding away at dangerous levels during his meetings. He had not realized until then how distressed he was by the daily scuffle of departmental politics, even when he felt uninvolved.

Without self-awareness, we are surprisingly oblivious to stress. Like the professor with heart problems or the laid-off workers, we allow stress to quietly creep in and dismantle our contentment. We allow it to sabotage our efforts and elongate our suffering. But once we diminish our blind spots, stress fades faster and keeps its distance more often.

2. Self-Awareness Strengthens Relationships

It all came to a head one day for Linda, a paralegal, as she sat alone in the work lunchroom for the third time that week. A year earlier she and a group of coworkers had always planned to take their lunches together. That half hour had been the highlight of her day since it was always filled with lively discussion. But lately her friends had been taking their lunches together, elsewhere—and they weren't inviting her.

On her drive home after work, Linda agonized, *Why? Don't my friends care about me anymore? What's wrong with them? Or is it me?*

What Linda didn't know is that she had been quietly poisoning her relationships over the past year until no one wanted to be around her anymore. When Janice, one of the women in the group, had become engaged, Linda was still single—and the only one who didn't congratulate Janice. Linda had made it clear, through her body language and sarcastic tone, that she didn't appreciate hearing about wedding plans or romantic dinners. And, most certainly, she didn't want to accompany the group on any shopping trips for bridal paraphernalia. Her bitterness had made her a difficult—and embarrassing—friend to be around. So as time went on, the group left her out of more and more activities.

It took a caring, kind, but firm pastor to help Linda identify her blind spots and uncover what she didn't even realize herself—that she considered herself half a person until she found "her other half." And that she was deeply angry at God because she had just turned forty and didn't yet have her soul mate.

Until Linda was able to acknowledge her blind spots and her hidden emotions, she could not be a real friend to Janice,

> Your paradigm is so intrinsic to your mental process that you are hardly aware of its existence, until you try to communicate with someone with a different paradigm.
> —DONELLA MEADOWS

who had been single for almost as many years and was excited but also nervous about linking her life permanently with another person.

If we are not self-aware—and on the road to becoming unswervingly authentic—it is impossible to step into another's shoes or to become a true friend. But as you become more aware of who you are and the factors that have influenced you, you can begin to work through those issues in your life. And that will leave you more time and emotional energy to improve your relationships.

3. Self-Awareness Unlocks Personal Freedom

When Oprah Winfrey was preparing to play Sethe in the movie *Beloved*, she arranged a trip along a portion of the Underground Railroad. "I wanted to connect with what it felt like to be a slave wandering through the woods," she said, "making the way north to a life beyond slavery—a life where being free, at its most basic level, meant not having a master telling you what to do every minute."

To immerse herself in the experience, Oprah was blindfolded and taken into the woods where she was left alone to contemplate how she would find her way to the next safehouse. "I understood for the first time that

> Let us resolve to be masters, not the victims, of our history, controlling our own destiny without giving way to blind suspicions and emotions.
>
> —JOHN FITZGERALD KENNEDY

freedom isn't about not having a master. Freedom is about having a choice."

The freedom to choose one's way in life is beyond compare. Without it, we are doomed to a life with limits at every turn. Consider Martha Chapman, a twenty-eight-year-old secretary to a grocery store buyer. Martha was convinced she'd soon be promoted to an assistant buyer, even though several younger women had been promoted ahead of her during the preceding three years. Martha's friends had been urging her to find a new job for years, but she turned down job offers, continuing to believe she had a future with the store. When her boss bluntly told her she was never going to be promoted, Martha was devastated.

"I had no idea at the time why I had been so blind to the truth," she recalls, "but I went into therapy because I felt absolutely worthless." Through therapy Martha realized that her blindness was rooted in unconscious fears. When she was a child, her father had moved the family across the country to take a new job. Soon afterward, he died of a heart attack.

"My father's death was a huge and horrible event in my childhood," Martha says, "but I didn't connect it with my own unwillingness to look for a better job in another company. In therapy, it became obvious to me that I associated my father's dying with his getting a new job and moving. In fact, I was unwilling to move too. For years I lived in a horrible one-room apartment in a crumbling neighborhood, telling my friends it had charm and character. I warped my life to avoid facing down my own fears, and I sacrificed my freedom to make my own choices."

If you feel stuck, stagnant, without options, then you've been boxed in by your blind spots. Once the blinders come off, a new perspective sets in. You see the horizon of possibilities. You recognize choices you didn't know you had. Self-awareness unlocks personal freedom.

> As iron sharpens iron, so one person sharpens another.
>
> —PROVERBS 27:17 NIV

How to Become More Self-Aware

While self-awareness can be heightened through a variety of means, the one we are about to reveal is the most fundamental and effective. Before we explore it, however, we have two important warnings.

1. Its effectiveness will either sink or swim based on your mind-set.

    The heightening of self-awareness demands a nonreactive, nonjudgmental attitude. It requires you to step back from your experience and explore it with an eagerness to accurately see it. Objectivity is the key. "A second self," says novelist William Styron, "is able to watch with dispassionate curiosity as his companion struggles." Are you up to this? Your mission is a direct seek-and-destroy attack on your own pockets of denial.

2. The nearer to the core of your personality you probe, the stronger your resistance will be.

But you *can* do it if you decide to. So we urge you to make a decision, at the outset, that you will pursue this path of finding the truth. If you don't want to find it, the strategy that follows will serve no purpose. If, on the other hand, you'd like to take this exciting journey of self-discovery, we are convinced it may be one of the most important things you ever do.

Hunting for your own blind spots is like trying to examine the back of your own head. You can arrange mirrors at just the right angle and contort your neck as much as you like, but the easiest solution is to *solicit feedback from others.*

We can almost feel some of you about to close the covers of this book. *I don't want to ask people for feedback,* you may be saying. But hear us out. The exercise we are about to outline just may be one of the single most important things you ever do to become healthy. It holds great potential for redefining you as a mature, well-balanced person.

Here it is. For the next week or so, ask one or two people every day (never asking the same person twice) a simple question: "Is there anything about me that I don't seem to see but you do?" You can ask it of family members as well as people on the periphery of your life. If you have the courage, you could even ask a relative stranger to give you their perception. Their insights might surprise you.

As you synthesize the information you're gathering,

consider two points: First, *brace yourself and be nondefensive.* Nobody likes feedback on their foibles. Hearing that you come off as aloof or insensitive can easily elicit a defensive emotional reaction. Curb this impulse by simply saying, "Thanks." You are on a fact-finding expedition, so don't launch into an argument, even if you think the person is off-base. You can decide later whether the person's feedback is useful.

Second, *make a plan for processing.* Sometimes feedback will be objective; other times the information may be viewed through that person's own lens and motives. One of the reasons for gathering feedback from several people is to filter out perceptions that have more to do with the speaker's dysfunction than yours. Typically, this feedback is vague—where the person can't think of an example to back it up. So ask for specific feedback, and if you deem it as useless, so be it. Let your gut tell you what is valuable.

Next, consider how you will use the feedback. Neurologist Oliver Sacks wrote about a man who, virtually blind from early childhood, had an operation that restored his sight when he was middle-aged. Though the man's eyes now took in visual information, his brain wasn't used to making sense of it. You may feel the same way as you consider this feedback. You're not used to

> Man's capacity to experience himself as both subject and object at the same time [is] necessary for gratifying living.
>
> —ROLLO MAY

your new set of eyes. So give it time. Don't expect to always correctly gauge how you are coming across to others as you work on being more sensitive or more assertive, for example. Be patient with yourself. You'll soon see your behavior more clearly as the false image of yourself gives way to a more accurate self-perception.

By the way, asking others for feedback can be an ongoing exercise. Six months after you initially receive feedback, you may want to go back to some of these same people and ask how they view you now. It's the only true way to track your progress. We have a friend who starts each new year with this exercise. During the first week of January, he mails out a simple feedback form to about ten people, asking them to point out his blind spots from the previous year. Incredibly intentional, right? You bet. And he's one of the most emotionally healthy people we know.

FOUR

Facing Your Fears
with Honesty

*It takes courage to grow up and
become who you really are.*

—E. E. CUMMINGS

artin Seligman was a twenty-one-year-old graduate student fresh out of college when he conducted
an experiment that set him on a quest to unravel why some
people lose courage, play it safe, give up, and remain passive
while others look for solutions, take risks, overcome fears, and
achieve results.

For the experiment, researchers taught dogs to associate a
tone with a very mild shock, the kind you get from touching

a doorknob on a wintery day. The dogs were restrained in a harness and then repeatedly exposed to the sound, followed by the shock. The hypothesis was that later, on hearing the same tone, the conditioned dogs would associate it with an oncoming shock and run or otherwise try to escape.

But what happened next was not expected.

Seligman and his associates placed an unrestrained dog inside a shuttle box, a container divided in half by a low wall. When the tone sounded, the dog could easily escape the discomfort of the mild shock by jumping over the wall into the other half of the box. But the researchers were stunned by the dog's response.

> Don't listen to those who say, you are taking too big a chance. Michelangelo would have painted the Sistine floor, and it would surely be rubbed out by today.
>
> —NEIL SIMON

On hearing the tone, instead of jumping away to the other side of the box, the dog lay down and began to whine. Even when the shock came, it did nothing to evade it. The researchers picked the whining dogs up to show them how easily they could escape. But when they were put back down, they did nothing. They tried the same with all the previously conditioned dogs. A full two-thirds of them didn't even try to escape the negative stimulus.

Seligman concluded that these dogs had "learned" to be helpless. In the early conditioning, they had received a shock no matter how much they barked or jumped or struggled; they learned that nothing they did mattered. So why try if you feel you can't win?

Have you ever felt like one of these dogs? Have you ever been tempted to give up because it appears little you did mattered?

If so, you're not alone.

Everyone, at some point, becomes like the dogs in Seligman's experiment. We all respond in a helpless manner on occasion because our experiences have taught us that we are not as strong as we thought we were. And when it comes to the ultimate human challenge—being true to ourselves—we give in to critics or buckle under the fear of not being able to fulfill our calling. So our faith fractures and our confidence warbles as we stay stuck in a proverbial comfort zone, where unswerving authenticity loses momentum and unfulfilled dreams go to die.

Stepping Outside Your Comfort Zone

A public opinion poll taken by the National Opinion Research Center found that over half of all adults ages eighteen to thirty-four rate their lives as "exciting." Once people reach their late thirties and forties, this lowers 1 percent to 50 percent. By age sixty-five it is at 49 percent. The Noble Prize–winning French philosopher, physician, and musician Albert Schweitzer fervently believed that "the tragedy of life is what dies inside a person while they live."

As the years slide by, far too many of us don't so much live as we merely exist. We play it safe, rarely venturing outside our emotional comfort zone. We trade passion for security. Is it a worthwhile trade? We don't think so. As we're about to show you, we think the strength and power that come from living with passion are worth the risk.

> We have to be honest about what we want and take risks rather than lie to ourselves and make excuses to stay in our comfort zone.
>
> —ROY T. BENNETT

If this is you, if you've been playing it safe—fearing what it would mean to live with unswerving authenticity—we hope you'll soon consider taking a bold step. It need not be big, just bold. Why? Because your dream, your true passion, is found just outside the boundary of your comfort zone. It's true for everyone. Dreams are never discovered in safety. They always require risk. Dreams are found and fulfilled in the unknown, in the frightful forest of Big Ideas. Without risking a venture into the unknown, we end up settling for a life we never would have predicted. But that doesn't have to be the case—no matter how far along life's journey you've traveled and no matter how daunting your dream may seem. You can live with unswerving authenticity when you face your fears with honesty.

To do just that, we want to challenge you with a brief exercise. Consider a set of concentric circles that look like this:

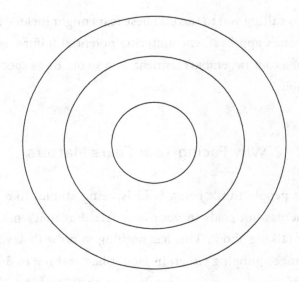

The innermost circle represents your emotional comfort zone. Note two or three things you're doing with your life right now that you'd consider safe. These are things that hold low or no risk. Fill the second circle with anything you might do with your life right now that you would classify as outside your immediate comfort zone. These are things you feel called to, but you keep putting off because critics or other reasons keep you from taking action. In the third circle, write at least one thing you've considered doing with your life, something that's still within your conscious thoughts, that is risky and bold.

Feel free to reproduce this diagram of the circles. Use a piece of paper and write out your answers. Once you've done that, note what fears keep pulling you back into your comfort zone and keep you from stepping onto the path

God is calling you to travel. These fears might include losing someone's approval, encountering potential failure, getting out of a routine, embarrassment, and so on. Be as specific as possible.

Why Facing Your Fears Matters

Some people think being bold is being stupid, like walking across hot coals in your bare feet. But that's not what we're talking about. This has nothing to do with skydiving or bungee jumping either. In fact, it has nothing to do with adrenaline or thrill-seeking. Facing your fears, for our purposes, is about uncovering your purpose and passion. It's about having enough courage to be true to yourself when it comes to following the path God wants you to travel. It's about transcending learned helplessness and following your calling with passion.

> Our life is composed greatly from dreams, from the unconscious, and they must be brought into connection with action. They must be woven together.
>
> —ANAÏS NIN

Solomon, that wise king, spent years of his life searching for passion. In the chronicle of that search, the book of Ecclesiastes, Solomon writes, "Whatever your hand finds to do, do it with all your might, for in the realm of the dead, where you are going, there is neither working nor planning nor knowledge nor wisdom" (9:10 NIV). People read that and think Solomon is saying, "Eat, drink, and be merry, for tomorrow you may die," but that's not it at all. He's saying, "Throw your whole heart into whatever you do. Live while you have the chance."

Nadine Stair got the message, if only too late. You may not know her name, but you may have heard about something the late Mrs. Stair, of Louisville, Kentucky, said when she was asked, at age eighty-five, what she would do if she had her life to live over again. She had a memorable answer:

"I'd dare to make more mistakes," she said. "I would relax. I would be sillier. I would take fewer things seriously. I would perhaps have more actual troubles and fewer imaginary ones. You see, I'm one of those people who lived seriously and sanely hour after hour, day after day. If I had it to do over again, I would take more chances. I would climb more mountains and swim more rivers."

Nadine goes on to say, "If I had to do it over again, I would travel lighter than I have. If I had my life to live over, I would start barefoot earlier in the spring and stay that way later in the fall. I would go to more dances. I would ride more merry-go-rounds. I would greet more people."

Ever feel like the days of your

> If you hear a voice within you saying, "You are not a painter," then by all means paint, boy, and that voice will be silenced.
>
> —VINCENT VAN GOGH

life have become too sensible, too sane—too safe? If so, you know that your dreams are lying dormant because of too much caution. As the German poet Johann Friedrich von Schiller said, "Who reflects too much will accomplish little." In other words, when we are overly cautious, we meander through our days with a malaise that keeps us waiting for our life to *really* begin. When our life is too controlled, too cautious, we lose our passion. We lose our sense of self.

Eileen Guder, author of *God, But I'm Bored!*, put it a bit more bluntly:

> You can live on bland food so as to avoid an ulcer; drink no tea or coffee or other stimulants, in the name of health; go to bed early and stay away from night life; avoid all controversial subjects so as never to give offense; mind your own business and avoid involvement in other people's problems; spend money only on necessities and save all you can. You can still break your neck in the bathtub, and it will serve you right.

Sure, it's a bit callous, but let's admit it: facing our fears with honesty and living boldly is not about playing it safe. You may not live on bland food. You may drink plenty of coffee. You may stay up late and be a bit reckless with your money. That's not the point, of course. Guder's message is directed to all of us who live encumbered with too much caution, never venturing beyond the emotional security of our self-imposed comfort zone.

Finding Your Path to Passion

We meet a lot of people who sigh deeply and say they're looking for their passion, something to set their souls on fire. But they never find it. Why? Because passion doesn't come from finding it "out there"; passion is an inside job.

Hear this: Passion does not produce commitment. Commitment produces passion. Once you give yourself to a person or a project, you *become* passionate. It's not the other way around. Your commitment fuels a devotion and a passion that lasts long after the average person has given up. Artist, scientist, and inventor Leonardo da Vinci possessed unquenchable passion—because of his commitment. "Obstacles cannot crush me," he said. "Every obstacle yields to stern resolve. He who is fixed to a star does not change his mind."

> [Learned helplessness is] the giving-up reaction, the quitting response that follows from the belief that whatever you do doesn't matter.
>
> —MARTIN SELIGMAN

A burning commitment lights the fire of passion. And passion reduces apathy to ashes. American writer Ella Wheeler Wilcox, in the first line of her poem "Will," said it nicely:

> There is no chance, no destiny, no fate,
> Can circumvent or hinder or control
> The firm resolve of a determined soul.

So where does this determination, this commitment, come from? One thing is certain: it's not born out of reward. Contrary to B. F. Skinner's famous theory of positive rein-forcement, which suggested that we perform better when we expect to get something out of it, psychologists now see that for long-lasting impact our behavior must stem from an *intrinsically* rewarding commitment.

James Garbarino of Loyola University Chicago asked sixth-grade girls to try to teach a new game to a younger child. He promised each girl a ticket for a free movie if she did a good job. He also asked another group of students if they'd like to try their hand at tutoring, but he said nothing to these girls about a reward. They would be doing it only because they volunteered to do so.

Garbarino wanted to know which group would teach more effectively. He found that those who were after the movie tickets took longer to communicate ideas, got frustrated more easily, and ended up with pupils who didn't understand the game as well as the children who learned from girls who were not promised a reward. Not only that, but the girls who were teaching without reward viewed the activity as something they would like to continue doing.

As Harvard University social psychologist Teresa Amabile put it, "We look to those extrinsic pressures and say, 'That must be why I'm doing this.'" We miss out on the mission. The fascination and enthusiasm for the cause mysteriously vanish along the way unless we're motivated by our own personal commitment.

We'll say it again: passion is an inside job. A burning commitment lights the fire of purpose and passion—and a soul on fire is what makes us bold. It's what causes us to face our fears and propels us forward when other people have given up. It's what keeps us going even after failure. It's what moves us ahead in the face of criticism or embarrassment.

The Risk-Taker's Advantage

Some people never come close to facing their fears or risk taking a bold step because they're waiting for a "lucky break." They think the life they long for is going to someday fall into their lap. You've known people who think life will begin once they get their promotion, or find someone to marry, or get out of debt, or whatever. And you already know that study after study shows that those who are extremely happy, those who are living their dream, usually have the same problems as everyone else, if not more serious ones. The difference? They've discovered the risk-taker's advantage.

The 1949 class of Harvard Business School graduates was stunningly successful. *Fortune* magazine dubbed them "the Class the Dollars Fell On." When these graduates were in their midfifties, a

> Life is either a daring adventure or nothing at all.
>
> —HELEN KELLER

landmark study revealed that some ranked high on a scale of well-being and demonstrated passion for living while others came in at the bottom of the scale and showed little contentment, let alone passion.

Compared to any other group of Americans of their age, this entire class had done exceptionally well, but some were still soured on life. They suffered from boredom in their work and seemed to feel they could have excelled in their careers even more. Their ego wound in their business life spread discontentment to their marriages, their relationships with their children, and their health.

When researchers probed the data to understand the dynamics of these unhappy people, they came to realize much of their despondency was due to a single quality. In fact, it was the most salient quality separating the two groups. The happiest group from this class had a willingness to risk change while the unhappy group resisted it. Two-thirds of them, in fact, said they would love to change what they did—but they didn't. The researchers' conclusion: "Even among men for whom a superior education has opened many doors, well-being is not easily sustained without a continuing willingness to risk change."

Don't misunderstand. The risk-taker's advantage is not about being impulsive or careless. It's about boldness, not bravado. Action, not arrogance. Risk, not recklessness. A calculated risk invigorates the soul and expands our life to become unswervingly authentic. "Man cannot discover new oceans," said French author André Gide, "unless he has the courage to lose sight of the shore."

We all have a shore that gives us security. It represents the comfortable and
easy part of our life that we know
well. What might happen if you
had the courage to lose sight of
the shoreline that keeps calling
you back from discovering new
oceans? And what might those
oceans be? Only you can answer. And
when you do, you're beginning to embody
the risk-taker's advantage.

> Fortune
> befriends
> the bold.
>
> —JOHN DRYDEN

The Secret to Overcoming Your Fears

One of the best anecdotes to overcoming any obstacle on
the road to fulfilling this dream was penned by a nineteen-
year-old sophomore in college, Kent Keith, back in 1968.
While attending Harvard College, Kent gave more than 150
speeches at high schools, student leadership workshops, and
student council conventions. Kent was providing an alterna-
tive student voice during the turbulent sixties, when student
activists were seizing buildings, throwing rocks at police,
and shouting down opponents. Kent encouraged students to
care about others and to work through the system to achieve
change.

But he soon learned that many students tended to give
up quickly when they faced difficulties or failures. They

needed deeper, longer-lasting reasons to keep trying. "I saw a lot of idealistic young people go out into the world to do what they thought was right, and good, and true," recalls Keith, "only to come back a short time later, discouraged, or embittered, because they got negative feedback, or nobody appreciated them, or they failed to get the results they had hoped for."

Kent told his fellow students that to change the world they had to love people—even when it wasn't easy. "The challenge is

> It is easy to be brave from a safe distance.
>
> —AESOP

to always do what is right and good and true, even if others don't appreciate it."

Pretty impressive words for a sophomore! But even more impressive is how he summarized his challenge. It came in the form of what he called the ten "Paradoxical Commandments." If you've heard them before, they're worth reading again. And again.

Here they are:

1. People are illogical, unreasonable, and self-centered. Love them anyway.
2. If you do good, people will accuse you of selfish ulterior motives. Do good anyway.
3. If you are successful, you win false friends and true enemies. Succeed anyway.

4. The good you do today will be forgotten tomorrow. Do good anyway.

5. Honesty and frankness make you vulnerable. Be honest and frank anyway.

6. The biggest men with the biggest ideas can be shot down by the smallest men with the smallest minds. Think big anyway.

7. People favor underdogs, but follow only top dogs. Fight for a few underdogs anyway.

8. What you spend years building may be destroyed overnight. Build anyway.

9. People really need help but may attack you if you do help them. Help people anyway.

10. Give the world the best you have and you'll get kicked in the teeth. Give the world the best you have anyway.

Today, Kent Keith continues to proclaim the message of these Paradoxical Commandments as a speaker and writer. And his powerful list has been spread far and wide, and often not credited to him. In fact, you may find Mother Teresa attached to these words. But she didn't write them.

Kent did.

Why the misplaced attribution? Most likely because Mother Teresa put them on the wall of her children's home in Calcutta. Imagine that. Even Mother Teresa, the icon of a bold dreamer of love, must have found it difficult on occasion.

Yet she did so anyway.

The First Step Is the Hardest

"A long journey begins with a single step." As clichés go, that's pretty wise. After all, facing your fears with honesty and being bold enough to step outside your comfort zone can sound scary. Why? Because being bold leads to the unknown. It requires a willingness to risk change. And everyone fears change. It is a fear rooted deep in our brains' physiology. That's why before we leave this chapter we've got to make this important point: Being bold and facing your fears does not require a "leap of faith." It asks only that you take the first step.

> Live daringly, boldly, fearlessly. Taste the relish to be found in competition—in having put forth the best within you.
>
> —HENRY J. KAISER

Inertia is the enemy of facing your fears and stepping on the path of unswerving authenticity. It causes us to wait for "someday." We wait for someday when the conditions are perfect, or someday when everyone agrees with us. Our fear looks for any reason to avoid being bold. The only cure for the inertia of waiting on "someday" is to take a small step now. Martin Luther King Jr. may have said it best: "Faith is taking the first step even when you don't see the whole staircase."

What does that first step look like for you? And what's keeping you from taking it? We pray you won't lie helpless like the dogs in the shuttle box of Martin Seligman's experiment.

One small step was all that was required for those discontented dogs to find freedom. And the same is true for you.

Dr. Seligman wrote his first paper on the phenomenon of learned helplessness shortly after earning his PhD in 1967, and he spent the rest of his life exploring it. He says it still amazes him that some people react just like most of the dogs in his laboratory when exposed to a fear, an obstacle, or a challenge. Some people give in to help-lessness, fearing they don't have what it takes to suc-ceed. They resign to their challenges and put off their dreams to stay stuck in living someone else's life, not theirs. Others show a bold and unflinching determination to rise above their fears. Their commitment inflames their passion and their passion moves toward their dreams along the path of unswerving authenticity, the road less traveled. The difference between them? Their decision to face their fears with honesty and take a bold step in the direction of their life's purpose.

> Love like you'll never get hurt. You've got to dance like nobody's watchin'.
>
> —SUSANNA CLARK AND RICHARD LEIGH

PART THREE

Self-Giving Love

If thou wishest to be loved, love.

—SENECA

I ask him that with both feet planted firmly on love, you'll be able to take in with all followers of Jesus the extravagant dimensions of Christ's love. Reach out and experience the breadth! Test its length! Plumb the depths! Rise to the heights! Live full lives, full in the fullness of God. . . .

I want you to get out there and walk—better yet, run!—on the road God called you to travel. I don't want any of you sitting around on your hands. I don't want anyone strolling off, down some path that goes nowhere. . . .

Pouring yourselves out for each other in acts of love, alert at noticing differences and quick at mending fences.

Ephesians 3:14–19; 4:1–3

In 1883 professor Henry Drummond began his famous lecture "The Greatest Thing in the World" by asking his college students a disarmingly simple question: "You have a life before you. Once only can you live it. What is the noblest object of desire, the supreme gift to covet?"

The rhetorical question required no reply. Everyone knew the answer: *love*. Self-giving love is the ultimate good. It lifts us outside ourselves. It helps us see beyond the normal range of human vision—and over walls of resentment and barriers of betrayal. Love rises above the petty demands and conflicts of life and inspires our spirit to give without getting. As the famous "love chapter" of the Bible says: "It always protects, always trusts, always hopes, always perseveres. . . . Love never fails" (1 Cor. 13:7–8 NIV).

When you set out on a consciously chosen course of action that accents the good of others, a deep change occurs in your soul. Pretentious egoism fades and your days are punctuated with spontaneous breathings of compassion and generosity, kindness and nurturance. Once you have laid claim to your profound significance and schooled yourself in the art of authenticity, your life is given to the *summum bonum*—the supreme good. The noblest of human qualities become your new compass on this "most excellent way."

Sound sappy? Science doesn't think so. Recent studies found that the ability to practice appreciation and love is the *defining* mark of the happiest of human beings. When people engage in self-giving love by doing something extraordinarily positive, they use higher-level brain functions and set off a series of neurochemical reactions that shower their systems in positive emotions.

Perhaps you are wondering if this kind of happiness is triggered just as readily by having fun as it is by an act of self-giving love. Martin Seligman, of the University of Pennsylvania, wondered the same thing. He gave his students an assignment: to engage in one pleasurable activity and one philanthropic activity and then to write about both. Turns out, the "pleasurable" activity of hanging out with friends, watching a movie, or eating a delicious dessert paled in comparison with the effects of the loving action. Seligman states that "when our philanthropic acts were spontaneous . . . the whole day went better." He goes on to say that self-giving love is not accompanied by a separable stream of positive emotion; rather "it consists in total engagement and in the loss of self-consciousness." Time stops when we lend a helping hand, nurture a hurting soul, or offer a listening ear.

If there is anything better than to be loved, it is loving—and healthy people know it. But as they aspire to the greatness of self-giving love, they do so with keen awareness and personal acknowledgment of their human limits. In the process of developing unswerving authenticity, they have realized that they have needs, drives, rights, and goals that do not easily harmonize with selfless love.

But does that mean they give up those needs, drives, rights, and goals? We want to be clear: love is not necessarily about self-denial. We have seen many well-intentioned people set out to "love" others by denying their own needs—as if performing a sacrifice was the goal. Not so. Healthy people know that self-giving love is not about doing without. As the greatest of love poems makes clear, we can give our bodies to be burned and still not be loving (1 Cor. 13:3). Self-giving love does not demand a titanic sacrifice. Small things, done with great love, most often characterize the actions of a person who is healthy and whole.

Love is the result of hundreds of small decisions, each and every day. Do I hurry to my next appointment or check in with a coworker who's hurting? Do I put my phone calls on hold to play with my five-year-old, or do I stick to my tasks to reduce my to-do list? Do I make the effort to warmly greet a visitor at church or rush to get to my normal seat? How we answer such small decisions determines how greatly we love. It determines how much we transcend our self to love without reward.

One of the most inspirational stories of self-giving love we have ever read is Mary Ann Bird's *The Whisper Test*. It's the story of a little girl who was different . . . and hated it. She was born with a cleft palate, and when she started school, her classmates made it clear to her how she looked: "A little girl with a misshapen lip, crooked nose, lopsided teeth, and garbled speech."

She was convinced that no one outside her family could love her. When her classmates asked, "What happened to your lip?" she'd tell them she'd fallen and cut it on a piece of glass. "Somehow," she wrote, "it seemed more acceptable to have suffered an accident than to have been born different."

There was, however, a teacher in the second grade whom all the students adored. Mrs. Leonard was short, round, and happy—"a sparkling lady." Annually, she administered a hearing test to everyone in the class. Finally, it was Mary Ann's turn.

> I knew from past years that as we stood against the door and covered one ear, the teacher sitting at her desk would whisper something, and we would have to repeat it back— things like, "The sky is blue," or "Do you have new shoes?" I waited there for those words that God must have put into her mouth, those seven words that changed my life. Mrs. Leonard said, in her whisper, "I wish you were my little girl."

Mrs. Leonard had a lock on love. You can be confident that she, like other healthy people, enjoyed the highest successes in living and the deepest levels of emotional satisfaction. Her tender care clearly embodied this hallmark of health—the *summum bonum*, the supreme good, the most excellent way.

And self-giving love is what this section of the book is all about. Truthfully, we have been eager for you to get to this point. For once you have experienced profound significance, really learned to cultivate and nurture your significance in the moments that make up each of your days, and once you have learned the secret of unswerving authenticity, really mastered your ability to sync your thoughts and feelings, you are primed to know the inexpressible joy of self-giving love. Significance and authenticity are the double doors to love.

Coming full circle, with our feet firmly planted on love, we begin to give God's love to others. How do we put this into practice? Two proven ways: we'll discuss in chapter 5 how we must learn to read our social barometer, and in chapter 6 how we must step into another person's shoes.

Every connection you have with another person—whether a friend, family member, or total stranger—is an opportunity to enjoy the pleasure of self-giving love. Every moment of every day that you are with another person is a chance to provide encouragement, support, and care. Self-giving love is a myriad of big and small acts of kindness and compassion, generosity and concern. When you begin living out these qualities, when they emanate from your core, emotional health and wholeness are at hand.

FIVE

Reading Your Social
Barometer

You can make more friends in two months
by becoming interested in other people
than you can in two years by trying to
get other people interested in you.

—DALE CARNEGIE

The "close talker."

If you were a fan of the 1990s television phenomenon
Seinfeld, you immediately understand that phrase. A certain
episode centered around a character who had little awareness
of personal space. Upon inviting you to join him for a cup
of coffee, he would stand within a couple of inches, putting

his face embarrassingly close to yours. The character later spawned episodes involving a "soft talker," who was barely discernible in conversation, and a "high talker," who said everything very loudly. Even if you weren't a fan of the show, chances are you still get the idea. Some people are just socially "off"—oblivious to their social morays.

Much of psychological health is internal. It has to do with your thoughts and feelings, your character and spirit. But there is a significant component of your well-being that is entirely other-focused. It has to do with your relationships and how you read other people's faces, understand their emotions, join them in conversation, and interpret their actions. It has to do with reading your "social barometer."

What do we mean by that? In 1643 an Italian scientist in Florence, Evangelista Torricelli, used a column of water in a three-foot tube to take the first-ever reading of barometric pressure. The column, soon replaced by mercury and reduced to a manageable size, has been used around the globe ever since by anyone wanting to forecast local weather. In the same way this device can predict climate conditions, your social barometer can become a reliable predictor of social conditions—if you know how to read it accurately.

Reading your social barometer attunes you to others. It creates a smooth interpersonal exchange that puts others at ease. It increases your social competencies, making you more adept at creating meaningful and enjoyable connections. Healthy people thrive in intimate relationships because they *can* read their social barometer. They thus develop a talent for rapport, building a web of social connection that enriches their lives. Healthy people rarely lack for friends.

Also, the healthier you are as an individual, the more adroit you become socially. By learning to read your social barometer, you lower your risk for coming off as arrogant, insensitive, or uninterested. Your social barometer will tell you when and how to enter a conversation midstream and when to lay low. It will tell you when to keep talking and when to clam up. It will prevent you from being oblivious to cues and hints that the conversation is shifting gears. And it tunes you in to attempts by others to refocus on another topic.

> The deepest principle in human nature is the craving to be appreciated.
>
> —WILLIAM JAMES

Without the ability to read your social barometer, you would be like a meteorologist trying to forecast weather conditions without knowing the barometric pressure. You would be at a loss, playing a social guessing game that's likely to miss the mark at any moment. For this reason, we dedicate this chapter to helping you mature, grow, and flourish in the world of interpersonal relationships. Consider this area another critical part of the foundation for personal health. Without it, not only do your relationships founder but so do you. Why? Because at the heart of who we are is a powerful motivation to be with others. The absence of human contact, research has clearly shown, leads to more mental and physical sickness and stress.

Contrary to what you might think, great friendships and romances do suddenly appear for a favored few. What some see as "fate" is more likely our own doing—or undoing. We determine the quality of our relationships because we can choose to read our social barometer—or not.

Finding Your Social Barometer

We are about to ask you a simple question. Before we do, however, we want you to know that how you answer this question will reveal whether you are already reading your social barometer. So take a contemplative moment to consider it. And be honest with yourself. Here's the question: *What thought races through your head when you walk into a room of people?*

While there are countless responses to this question, all of them are likely to fall into one of two basic camps. These two fundamental responses, in our experience, come in the form of two quiet questions:

1. How am I doing?
2. How are they doing?

Any social setting fundamentally elicits one of these two positions. When you walk into a room full of other people, either you are concerned with yourself and the impression you are about to make or you are focused on them and what is taking place.

Whenever your approach falls into the category of *How are they doing?* you have found your social barometer.

Alternatively, when your basic social approach is to ask *How am I doing?* you are relating without valuable interpersonal information that only your social barometer can give.

Relating to others without reading your social barometer is like wearing mirrored sunglasses with the lenses flipped around. You look out at the world and all you see reflects yourself, your own needs, your own desires. Your self-focus is preventing you from accurately recognizing other people's needs and desires as well as their motives and emotions. The point is this: without your social barometer you are destined to be consumed by self-conscious behavior that will riddle your relationships with social insecurity.

> You're blessed when you care. At the moment of being "care-full," you find yourselves cared for.
>
> —MATTHEW 5:7

Almost all of us have moments when we are emotionally strong and steady. And then there are other moments, in the very same day, when we are out of sync, self-conscious, and unsure. But the healthy person is still dedicated to tuning in to their social barometer. They have disciplined themselves to enter a room and ask themselves, *How are these people doing?*

Reading Your Social Barometer

A person who has experience reading their social barometer sees interpersonal cues that the untrained eye repeatedly misses. They scan the social scene for important details to guide their actions. Not only do they listen to the *words* being spoken, they observe the person's nonverbals. They pay attention to voice tone, facial expressions, and eye contact. They recognize a nervous fidget. When they shake someone's hand, they take note of the feel of the handshake. They recognize an uncomfortable shift of weight in a chair. They are tuned in to unspoken feelings and are sensitive to signals that convey a person's interest.

> No one can make you feel inferior without your consent.
>
> —ELEANOR ROOSEVELT

How important is it to read your social barometer accurately? Researchers believe that about 90 percent of emotional communication is nonverbal. And studies like Robert Rosenthal's back up this estimate. Rosenthal, a psychology professor at the University of California, helped develop an assessment of people's ability to read emotional cues. It's called the Profile of Nonverbal Sensitivity (PONS). He shows subjects a film of a young woman expressing feelings like anger, jealousy, love, and gratitude. Unbeknownst to the viewer, one or another nonverbal cue has been edited out. In some instances, the face is visible but not the body. Or the woman's eyes are hidden, so the viewers must judge the feeling by subtle cues. Interestingly enough, people with higher PONS scores, even if their IQs are quite average, tend to be more well liked and more successful in their work and relationships.

Reading one's social barometer is not only about recognizing the cues that others are sending, however. It's also about seeing signs in oneself. A healthy person, while other-focused in social settings, pays close attention to their own internal psychological experiences as a means to improving relational connections. They are aware of even subtle feelings as they have them.

To avoid any confusion on this point, look at it this way. The person asking *How am I doing?* is looking for external validation. This validation is an end in itself. They mistakenly believe that if somebody is affirming them in some way, if they win someone's approval, they are now more worthwhile. Self-respect and significance, as we have said already, can never be grounded in external validation like this. So don't confuse this internal focus of reading one's social barometer with such a self-deceptive approach. No. The healthy person is tuned in to their own experience with others not to find validation but as a means to more effective relating.

Why We Become Socially Insecure

"I never feel at ease, whether it's on the job or at a family reunion. I'm always anxiety-ridden and worried that someone is looking at me, and I don't measure up. Whenever I must make a team report at work, I get a lump in my throat and my mouth gets dry. Whenever I'm in a social setting, I feel self-conscious and insecure."

Ever felt that way? Do you know someone who does? Millions and millions of good-hearted people are in the grip of social insecurity. While it may not paralyze their relationships, it certainly suffocates their efforts. They may want to join a conversation but withdraw out of fear. Conversely, they may boldly enter in and then wish they hadn't. Their social insecurity makes relating to others often nerve-racking and sometimes painful.

> A person who is shut out, who feels unwanted, unloved . . . brings a people to be spiritually poor, and that is the worst poverty and the most difficult to overcome.
>
> —MOTHER TERESA OF CALCUTTA

Why do so many people suffer socially? Those in the know point to several predictable pitfalls. So before we delve into the ins and outs of becoming more socially competent, let's take a look at each of these pitfalls.

Pitfall 1: Comparing Ourselves to Others

"In the misfortune of our best friends there is something that does not entirely displease us." François de La Rochefoucauld, the seventeenth-century French essayist who wrote these words, must certainly have suffered from social insecurity. Every human being feels sorry when something bad happens to someone we care for; but for the insecure, another's misfortune is a means of feeling better about themselves.

What the insecure person does not realize is that their very compulsion to measure their status against others is what is feeding their insecurity. With each comparison they diminish their potential to become intrinsically stronger and more stable on their own.

Now let's be honest: everyone, no matter how healthy, occasionally pulls out the proverbial yardstick to compare their performance and their achievements to others'. It's only natural. But the person entrenched in social insecurity is forever comparing themselves. It is their main means to feeling worthwhile—and that's why they rarely do. Social comparison inevitably leads to feelings of bitterness. There will always be someone who has more than you, makes more than you, does better than you, and feels better than you. Always. Still, some choose to torture themselves by comparing themselves to others, and the result is hollow vanity at best—but most likely feelings of inferiority.

Pitfall 2: Shyness

It is a nearly universal human trait. Most everyone has bouts of shyness, and half of all people describe themselves as shy. Perhaps because it is so widespread and conveys a sense of vulnerability, shyness can be viewed as endearing. There is nothing inherently wrong with shyness—not until a person feels imprisoned by it. Once shyness engenders excessive self-consciousness, to the point of preventing connections, it crosses a dangerous line.

Harvard professor emeritus Jerome Kagan has shown that by eight weeks of age babies display innate shyness or boldness. Yet many shy babies become gregarious ten-year-olds, and some outgoing babies become shy adults. This tells us that while a genetic predisposition plays a role in our timidity, shyness need not cripple our relationships. There are many steps the shy can take to develop satisfying relationships without violating their basic nature (many of which we point out later in this chapter), but when one categorically dismisses the possibility of social competence because of their shyness, they are making a big mistake. This will inevitably lead to a level of shyness that borders on social phobia, where they will barely utter a sentence without obsessing over the impression they are making.

> You're blessed when you're content with just who you are—no more, no less.
>
> —MATTHEW 5:5

Pitfall 3: Sensitivity to Criticism

No matter how hard you work, how great your ideas, or how wonderful your talent, you will be the object of criticism. Even the perfect motives of Jesus were often misunderstood, resulting in malicious criticism. No one is exempt. And how you respond to criticism will play a major role in your sense of security.

Consider Walt Disney. He was bankrupt when he went around Hollywood with his little "Steamboat Willie" cartoon idea. Can you imagine Disney trying to sell a talking mouse with a falsetto voice in the days of silent movies? Disney's dreams were big, and he had plenty of critics. People closest to him, however, believe Disney thrived on criticism. He was said to have asked ten people what they thought of a new idea, and if they were unanimous in their rejection of it, he would begin work on it immediately.

A single critical comment, for many, is enough to shut down all sources of creativity. Few among us thrive on it like Walt did. But on the other end of the continuum are those whose sensitivity to criticism creates a social stalemate. They stymie all progress for fear of someone saying something critical. Sir Isaac Newton is said to have been so sensitive to criticism that he withheld the publication of a paper on optics for fifteen years, until his main critic died.

Pulitzer Prize–winning journalist Hebert Bayard Swope once noted: "I can't give you the formula for success, but I can give you the formula for failure: try to please everybody all the time." The person who is overly sensitive to criticism is trying to do just that. No wonder they feel socially insecure.

The Fundamental Social Skill

If you have avoided the common pitfalls of social insecurity and are becoming more tuned in to reading your social barometer, you are primed to focus on a single skill that the socially competent continually master. This single skill may be the most important thing you can do for making meaningful connections and for understanding and carrying out the principles of self-giving love. Its simplicity, if not studied, causes it to go unnoticed. But once you recognize its power, you will never approach a relationship without it. The skill? Asking a string of quality questions.

In 1936 the grandfather of all people-skills books was published. It was an overnight hit, eventually selling more than fifteen million copies. And today that book, *How to Win*

> He has achieved success who has lived well, laughed often and loved much; who has gained the respect of intelligent men and the love of little children; . . . who has never lacked appreciation of earth's beauty or failed to express it; who has always looked for the best in others and given the best he had; whose life was an inspiration.
>
> —BESSIE A. STANLEY

Friends and Influence People by Dale Carnegie, is just as useful as it was when it was first published. Why? Because Dale Carnegie understood that human nature will never be outdated, and he knew how to ask quality questions. The skills he teaches in this classic book are undergirded by a pervasive principle: people crave to be known and appreciated.

Quality questions are intentionally designed to open up a person's spirit. They aren't throwaway questions, like, "How about those Red Sox?" or, "Can you believe this weather?" though those types of questions certainly have their place.

Quality questions invite vulnerability but are not invasive. They are personal but respect privacy. They are asked out of genuine interest but never blunt. A quality question conveys kindness, warmth, concern, and interest. It is couched in affirmation and appreciation.

Here's an example. Not long ago, the two of us were in Dallas, Texas, to speak at a conference. The host assigned to pick us up at the airport was waiting outside security with our names on a placard.

"Howdy, my name is J. T.," he said as he reached to carry a suitcase or two. We hopped into his vehicle and were on our way—until we hit rush-hour traffic. We were at a near standstill for nearly two hours, and that gave us plenty of time to talk.

"Tell us about your hobbies, J. T. What do you do for fun?" we asked.

He became animated as he told us about playing racquetball.

"Sounds like you really enjoy it," one of us followed up, "and I bet you get plenty of exercise."

"Oh, yes," he replied, and then he went into describing the competition he entered last year and how he fared.

"You really love it, don't you?" we said.

"It's not only fun; you're exactly right about it keeping me in shape." J. T. then told us about his father's triple bypass surgery two years ago.

As the traffic crawled, we asked J. T. about his work.

"I love computer programming," he told us.

> The applause of a single human being is of great consequence.
>
> —SAMUEL JOHNSON

"I bet there's a story behind you getting into that field," we said.

J. T. told us about a high school teacher who mentored him and how his father loved to tinker with electronics. J. T. then described several of his projects.

With plenty of time on our hands, we were able to ask J. T. questions about his family. Questions about his church. Questions about his upbringing. We asked literally dozens of questions.

And you know what? When we finally pulled up to our hotel and began unloading our bags, J. T. said, "You two sure are interesting. It was great getting to know you." And with that he climbed into his SUV and sped away.

We looked at each other and smiled.

Truth be told, J. T. didn't get to know us at all. In two hours of conversation, he literally did not ask a single question except for the obligatory "How was your flight?" It's not an uncommon experience. Many people who have never found their social barometer don't know how to put the spotlight on the person they are with. They've never consciously considered how to pull a person out and make them feel known.

The only reason J. T. thought we were interesting is because we showed genuine interest in him. And we affirmed him on top of it. For nearly two hours, he was on center stage with two strangers who supplied him with a string of quality questions about himself. That kind of genuine interest had succeeded in making him feel good about himself as he sped off.

Perhaps you are already aware of the power of this simple strategy. Maybe you have been doing it for years. Then congratulations! We are sure you don't lack for friends.

But if you are unsure about your social barometer, it's time to act if you want to become the kind of person who radiates self-giving love. If you sometimes endure too many conversational lulls or feel socially awkward too frequently or if you suffer from shyness, why not give this a try?

Take a colleague to lunch and begin a line of quality questions. We're convinced you will sense a new level of social confidence almost immediately. As you think in terms of *How are they doing?* and choose to be genuinely interested, you will witness how quickly this person feels understood and appreciated. But be prepared. If the person is socially unskilled, like J. T., the questions will be one-sided. You will be doing most (or all) of the question asking; the other person will be doing most of the talking.

If, on the other hand, they are reading their own social barometer, they will eventually turn the tables. And you will witness the social law of reciprocity that states, "Vulnerability begets vulnerability." Once they reveal information about their career aspirations, for example, they will be genuinely interested in yours. And when this kind of give-and-take occurs on nearly any subject, you will find yourself in the midst of a terrific conversation. You are enjoying emotional rapport and social synchrony—and building a stronger relationship.

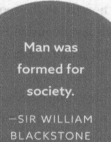

Man was formed for society.

—SIR WILLIAM BLACKSTONE

The Fruit of a Healthy Relationship

When two healthy people (both tuned in to their social barometers) get together, it's like drinking lemonade in the desert. They breathe a collective sigh. They relax. They can be who they are, and they know that just being together will restore their spirits. Why? Because some things—what we call the fruit of a healthy relationship—are certain. In a healthy relationship, you can count on, at the very least, these qualities: confidentiality, honesty, and personal space.

Fruit 1: Confidentiality

A Jewish publication ran an advertisement dominated by a drawing of a very stern-looking bearded rabbi of the nineteenth century, the Chofetz Chaim, who wrote a book about gossip called *Guard Your Tongue*. At the bottom of the page was a hotline number to call anonymously if you had information about someone's potential marriage, business dealings, or whatever. A rabbi at the other end would tell you whether your gossip was important enough to pass along. If not, you were counseled to guard your tongue.

Interesting, isn't it? The advertisement reveals as much about the state of our relationships as it does about our propensity for gossip. Who among us hasn't been hurt by a broken confidence? It usually begins when your friend says to someone: "You have to promise you won't tell Brenda I told you this because she made me swear not to tell anyone . . ." It sounds very confidential. But then why are they telling you the secret? They appear to be keeping a secret but aren't. Jesus understood this when he said, "Whatever you have spoken in the dark will be heard

> Lonely people talking to each other can make each other lonelier.
>
> —LILLIAN HELLMAN

in the light, and what you have spoken in the ear in inner rooms will be proclaimed on the housetops" (Luke 12:3 NKJV).

We've all shared private and personal information with a trusted friend, only to learn later that our friend has blabbed it to the world. But does this mean we can't expect *anyone* to keep their mouth closed? No. Not if they're healthy. We *need* to tell our secrets. It helps us explore what's troubling us and sometimes leads to helpful feedback. Sharing our secrets lets us test the reaction to what we've been holding in our heart. Not only that, it's a relief not to be the only person who has experienced a certain temptation or tragedy. It makes us feel less alone when we unburden our soul and a friend says, "Me too," or, "I understand." Sharing a secret can bring us closer together and deepen our relationship—but only if the relationship is healthy. Healthy people consider it a privilege to hear what's on our mind, and they leave it at that. When it comes to keeping a confidence, healthy people are a human vault.

Fruit 2: Honesty

"Genuine relationships cannot possibly exist where one of the parties is unwilling to hear the truth," says Cicero, "and the other is equally indisposed to speak it." As painful as the truth might be, a healthy relationship cannot survive without it. As the well-known proverb says, "A friend loves at all times, and a brother is born for adversity" (Prov. 17:17 NKJV). Now this does not mean that honesty gives license to be insulting, offensive, or badgering. Healthy relationships call for speaking the truth in love and respect. Without these ingredients, honesty is a lethal weapon. Perhaps that's what caused Cicero to add, "Remove respect from friendship and you have taken away the most splendid ornament it possesses."

People deserve the respect of knowing the truth. They deserve to know if they are hurting someone's feelings, being too aggressive, too lazy, too anything. And healthy people know they can't live without this kind of feedback. Without it they cannot achieve unswerving authenticity, as we discussed earlier in this book, or understand themselves well enough to be able to empathize with others and extend self-giving love freely, without conditions or restraints.

> No act of kindness, however small, is ever wasted.
>
> —AESOP

Some time ago I (Les) was counseling a twentysomething student named Lisa, who came to my office in hopes of resolving a problem with a close friend. Lisa wasted no time in telling me the problem concerned her friend's stinginess.

"Jenny is so tight, she squeaks when she walks," Lisa confessed.

"Is this a new problem?" I asked.

"Oh no, it's been going on for years. But it's really wearing thin, and I find myself wanting to avoid being with Jenny whenever money is involved."

Lisa went on to tell me how meticulous Jenny can be when trying to figure out a shared bill at a restaurant. She told me about the time it took an extra ten minutes to pay for parking at a downtown garage because she wanted to make change for splitting the bill.

"How does Jenny respond when you talk to her about being so stingy?"

"Talk to her?!" she exclaimed. "I've never brought the subject up. I don't want to hurt her feelings."

Lisa and I spent the next several minutes exploring how much she valued her relationship with Jenny. Turns out, they were "best friends." But here she was, on the brink of tossing away an eight-year friendship because she didn't want to hurt Jenny's feelings. In other words, the one friendship she cared more about than any other was about to go under because she couldn't speak the truth.

Fortunately, with a little advice and coaching, Lisa mustered up the courage to confront Jenny on this annoying habit and the problem began to slowly reverse itself. The point to be learned here is that friends who do not care enough to confront may save themselves a little awkwardness in the present, but they will end up losing their friendships in the future. A healthy relationship is built on honesty.

Healthy people aren't afraid to be honest, and they aren't afraid to be themselves. They follow Emerson's advice: "Better be a nettle in the side of your friend than his echo." Translation: speak the truth, because if you are afraid of making enemies, you'll never have good friends.

Fruit 3: Personal Space

Emotionally needy people don't understand the meaning of space. They mother and smother us with their very presence. Their constant connecting becomes oppressive—if not possessive. This kind of person has no appreciation for what C. S. Lewis meant when he said: "In each of my friends there is something that only some other friend can fully bring out." In other words, Lewis recognized the need for space in a healthy relationship. He saw the need for multifaceted relationships that help us shine where another friend, even a close one, simply is not able. This is one of the marks of a space-giving relationship: each person relinquishes a possessive hold to enable the cultivation of other relationships.

Along this same line, a healthy relationship respects serenity. It recognizes the value of a thoughtful silence and a private retreat. Philosopher and author Henry David Thoreau said, "I never found the companion that was so companionable as solitude." Let's face it: There are times in everyone's life when we need to be alone. Times when we need to gather our wits and allow our souls to catch up. Healthy people understand this. Part of self-giving love means that we provide space, when needed, for the companion of solitude to

> Let there be spaces in your togetherness.
>
> —KAHLIL GIBRAN

enter a relationship. Of course, we also know when to return, break the silence, and rejoin the other person's journey.

All of us need space for the companion of solitude but, even more, we need to be in relationship. After all, it is this very space and separation provided by a healthy relationship that draws us back to a full appreciation of the relationship.

We hope you've come to understand more about your own social barometer—and how to read it—through this chapter. We've explained why the healthier you are, the healthier your relationships become. Which brings us back to the question we started this chapter with: Are you a "close talker"? Are you emotionally tone deaf to others? Are you ever accused of talking too much or being too reserved? The good news, as you have just seen, is that social competence can be learned. More important, as you become psychologically healthier, the social skills of tuning in to others come more naturally, and you eventually focus not on the skills it requires but on the needs and concerns of those around you. In other words, you are focused, in time, on self-giving love.

SIX

Stepping into
Another's Shoes

If there is any one secret of success, it lies
in the ability to get the other person's point
of view and see things from that person's
angle as well as from your own.

—HENRY FORD

L isten to this," Les said. We were sitting on an airplane and
he pulled the fold-down tray from the back of the seat in
front of him. With wide eyes full of expectancy looking at me,
he began tapping on the tray with his index finger.

I listened for a moment, obviously puzzled. He just kept
tapping and looking at me.

"Have you lost your mind?" I asked as I put my magazine down.

"I'm tapping a song. Can you guess what it is?" Les kept tapping as I only half-heartedly played along. "Come on, you can get this," he said.

That's when a curious passenger next to me, who had been completely quiet up to this point of the trip, piped up: "Is it Morse code?"

Les, suddenly self-conscious, terminated his tapping.

"Seriously, what's that all about?" I asked.

Les insisted it was a song and revealed that he'd been reading about a research project at Stanford University that compelled him to try the experiment on me.

The study was unusually simple. Elizabeth Newton, a doctoral student, assigned people to one of two roles: "tappers" or "listeners." Tappers received a list of a couple dozen well-known songs, such as "Happy Birthday to You," "Mary Had a Little Lamb," and "The Star-Spangled Banner." Then, after selecting one of the songs, their task was to tap out the rhythm to a listener by knocking on a table. The listener's job was to decipher the rhythm being tapped and guess the song.

Pretty simple, right? Well, as it turns out, the listener's job is quite difficult—as

> The heart has its reasons, which reason does not know.
>
> —BLAISE PASCAL

the curious plane passenger and I soon discovered. Over the course of Newton's experiment, 120 songs were tapped out. Listeners guessed only 2.5 percent of the songs. That's just 3 correct guesses out of 120!

So what's this atypical doctoral dissertation have to do with trading places? Plenty. Here's what makes the results of Elizabeth Newton's study worthy of an advanced degree. Before the listeners guessed the name of the song, Newton asked the tappers to predict the odds that their listeners would guess correctly. The tappers predicted that their listeners would be right 50 percent of the time. In other words, tappers thought they were getting their message across one time in two. But, in fact, their message was getting across only one time in forty.

Why? Because when a tapper taps, she is *hearing* the song in her head. The tapping seems obvious to her. She can't help but hear it as she taps, and she therefore believes the listener has a very good chance of deciphering her tune. Try it yourself. Tap "Happy Birthday to You." It's impossible to avoid hearing the tune as you do so. And when your listener guesses "Mary Had a Little Lamb," you wonder, *How could you be so stupid?*

Of course, the listener is not stupid. Not knowing what the tune is, he only hears a bunch of disconnected taps that resemble chicken pecks more than a musical number. But to the informed tapper, he comes off as dim-witted.

The same thing happens in our relationships. When we "tap out" our message—whether it's with our words, our inflection, or our body language—we believe it should be relatively obvious to our listener. But it's not. Sometimes a seemingly evident message isn't evident at all. It's far from obvious if you're not in the know.

That's where the power of empathy comes in. Once you hone your empathic abilities, you will "tap" differently. What's more, you'll "listen" differently. In fact, when you harness the power of empathy in your relationships, you'll enjoy connections that are deeper and better than ever.

We've been studying empathy for decades. Literally. We speak about it from stage, on the airwaves, and in our writing. We began doing research on empathy while we were in graduate school more than two decades ago, and we still haven't come close to exhausting the topic. I, Les, conducted a massive study on the topic and wrote my doctoral dissertation on empathy. And a few years ago we wrote a book, *Trading Places*, devoted to the science and practice of empathy. In many ways what you are about to read in this chapter is a summary of our most salient findings and conclusions over all these years about how to accurately walk in another person's proverbial moccasins.

What It Means to Empathize

Let's define what we're talking about. *Empathy* means imagining what life is like at a moment in time for another person. It means putting yourself in their skin, looking at life through their eyes. It means walking in their shoes. And it's a rarity.

Only the healthiest people among us become adept at practicing empathy. And that's exactly why their relationships are healthy too. Empathy is the on-ramp to self-giving love. It's the single most important skill set for your relationships. And everything you've read in this book has been leading to this. Empathy is the evidence of self-giving love.

The point of empathy is to understand another's feelings, desires, ideas, and actions at a meaningful level. In a sense, its goal is to momentarily *become* the other person. It's what poet Walt Whitman was getting at back in 1855 when he wrote his masterwork, *Leaves of Grass*: "I do not ask how the wounded one feels; I, myself, *become* the wounded one."

One dictionary defines *empathy* as "the identification with and understanding of another's situation, feelings, and motives." But what it doesn't tell you is how easily empathy can be mistaken for much less than this. And it doesn't tell you that empathy requires two sides.

Here's the secret most miss: empathy calls for loving other people with both your head and heart, concurrently. Most of us do one or the other well; we either feel someone's pain with our hearts or we try to solve their problem with our heads. To do both can be tricky. But that's the request of empathy.

> Love your neighbor as yourself.
>
> —JESUS, IN MATTHEW 22:39 NKJV

Think about it. When you trade places with another person, when you truly empathize with him or her, you are using both your analytical skills and your sympathetic skills. In short, you're using both your head and your heart.

Most people never understand the implications of this insight. You see, some of us are programmed to "empathize" intellectually, using our heads to analyze someone's circumstances. I (Les) do this whenever I nobly spell out Leslie's issues by saying things like "If you didn't get so emotional about this problem, you might just see that it's not that bad." Is this objective observation true? It may be. But it's not empathy. And in most cases, it's not even helpful.

Others of us are more inclined to "empathize" emotionally, using our hearts to sympathize with someone's position. I (Leslie) do this with compassion and sensitivity, when I sidle up to Les and say things like "I know you're feeling discouraged and I really hurt for you." Is this subjective surveillance accurate? Perhaps. Les may indeed be feeling discouraged. But maybe not. And in either case, it's not empathy.

Both approaches are pale imitations, mere masquerades of empathy. But know this: when these two approaches come together, true empathy takes flight. Like two wings of an airplane, empathy requires both your head and your heart before it can get off the ground.

When we attempt to "love" others primarily with our heads, we are merely analyzing. And when we "love" with our hearts, we are merely sympathizing. Of course, there's nothing wrong with either. But don't mistake them for empathy.

Empathy requires a deep emotional attunement tempered by an objective cognitive capacity. That's the key. It's a tall order, no doubt. That's why it's built on the foundation of profound significance and unswerving authenticity.

What Empathy Does for Your Relationships

What exactly do you get when you enroll empathy in the service of your relationships? Plenty. Sound too good to be true? It's not. Major research studies in recent years have revealed incredible rewards for those who practice empathy. Let's take a look at just a few that top the list.

Empathy Curbs Criticism

While taking a shower, Kansas City pastor Roy Bowen had an idea. Tired of hearing people complain about every detail in his church services, he asked his flock to take a pledge: vowing not to complain, criticize, gossip, or use sarcasm for twenty-one days. He gave everyone who agreed a purple bracelet as a reminder to curb their complaining— asking them to switch it to the other wrist if they caught themselves complaining—and then restart counting the days.

> I try to hear things through the ears of others, and see things through their eyes.
>
> —LEONARD RIGGIO

Pretty good idea, huh? After all, who wouldn't like to eliminate complaining? Well, a little-known secret among relationship specialists is the fact that complaining is good for your marriage. You read that right! It's good for your close relationships. Research at the University of Washington has shown that complaining, at a moderate level, helps couples and close friends air their grievances and keep improving. What isn't helpful is criticism.

So what's the difference between criticism and complaining? Criticism almost always begins with *you* ("You always make us late!"). Whereas complaining almost always begins with *I* ("I feel so frustrated when we are late to something that matters to me"). This may seem like a small matter of semantics, but it makes a big difference in your relationships.

And when you practice empathy, you automatically curb your criticism. And you don't even have to wear a purple bracelet to do so. All you need to do is see your complaint from the other person's point of view. That's what converts an obnoxious criticism ("You never turn off the lights") to a more receptive complaint ("I wonder if you could turn off that light when you're done in the garage").

Empathy Shortens Your Conflicts

Let's face it. Conflict is inevitable. We can argue about the silliest little things: "Who took my pen?" or "You just passed a parking space right there!" Such seemingly innocuous questions and statements, when augmented with a particular attitude, can ignite a major blowout. It's almost unavoidable. We can't eliminate conflict completely—not if we are being authentic with our feelings. But empathy can reduce conflict's lifespan and minimize its negative impact.

How does empathy do this for us? By trading in the blame game for positive solutions. It exchanges "you" statements for "we" statements. A study reported in *Psychological Science* discovered that the "best" arguers are those who don't point their fingers, and the person who says "we" the most during an argument suggests the best solutions.

> The great gift of human beings is that we have the power of empathy.
>
> —MERYL STREEP

In the study, researchers from the University of Pennsylvania and the University of North Carolina at Chapel Hill concluded, "'We' users may have a sense of shared interest that sparks compromise and other ideas. 'You'-sayers, on the contrary, tend to criticize, disagree, justify, and otherwise teem with negativity."

In other words, when you empathize with a friend, a spouse, or a colleague, you make conflict inclusive. It eliminates finger-pointing, taking the focus off a person to blame and moving it onto the problem to be solved. Like we said, it exchanges "you" statements for "we" statements.

Empathy Infuses Your Relationships with Grace

Shlomo Carlebach, a Jewish rabbi and musician, taught that experiences of God can never be planned or achieved. "They are spontaneous moments of grace, almost accidental."

One of his students once asked, "Rabbi, if God-realization is just accidental, why do we work so hard doing all these spiritual practices?"

The rabbi replied, "To be as accident-prone as possible."

The same is true of spontaneous moments of grace—those moments when we replace condemnation with undeserved love. You see, the more we practice empathy, the more likely grace is to infuse our relationships.

I've seen it firsthand. In fact, there is a legendary story in our home about an incident that happened a few years ago. I (Leslie) did something that would have been catastrophically worse had it not been for a healthy dose of grace from Les. I was running errands in our car, and since our youngest had fallen asleep in his car seat, I decided to drop him off back home with my husband. Then my errands could go more quickly, and I wouldn't disturb Jackson's slumber.

I'd pulled our car in to our

> It is only as we fully understand opinions and attitudes different from our own and reasons for them that we better understand our own place in the scheme of things.
>
> —S. I. HAYAKAWA

garage, opened the back-seat door, struggled to finagle Jack out of his safety harness without waking him, and carried my baby upstairs. "Les," I told my husband, who was working in his study, "I'm leaving Jack with you while I do some grocery shopping. He's asleep in his crib."

Les acknowledged my plan as I hurried back to the garage and jumped back into the car. But as I pulled out of the garage, a noise I'll describe as "unsettling" rang through our neighborhood. Turns out I'd forgotten to close the back-seat door after taking little Jackson out of his car seat. As I pulled out of the garage, the open door smacked the side of our garage door and ripped both doors clean off.

Les flew down the stairs in an instant, wide-eyed, to see me crying as I sat behind the wheel. The cause of this car accident was obvious. I gripped the wheel, bracing myself for what Les was about to say. But he didn't holler. He didn't lay blame. He kissed me on the cheek and said, "I was thinking we needed a new car door, so this is perfect."

Of course, I didn't deserve that kind of grace in that moment. My thoughtlessness not only cost us money, it meant we wouldn't be driving the next day on our long-awaited ski trip. But instead of guilt, condemnation, and anger, I got grace. Why? As Les said that evening over dinner, "If I were in your shoes in that moment, the last thing I would have needed from you was to be scolded."

You've heard the Native American proverb, "Do not judge your neighbor until you have walked two moons in his moccasins." Well, that certainly rings true when you practice empathy. Because you've walked in another's shoes, judgment is replaced by grace.

Empathy Is Fast-Acting

Now that we've noted a few of the relationship rewards that come from empathy, you need to know that this happens quickly. If you've been taking the steps we've been prescribing in this book, if you've been working to put them into practice, we've got good news. We want you to know that the rewards of empathy come far quicker than you think.

> Trying to observe the slow shift from self-centeredness to empathy is like trying to watch grass grow.
>
> —NEAL MAXWELL

Don't believe us? Consider this: In the 1930s, American Airways, which later became American Airlines, had a tremendous problem with lost luggage. Passenger complaints kept coming even after the company tried their best to get their station managers to overcome the problem. Finally, LaMotte Cohn, general manager of the airline at the time, came up with an idea. Cohn asked all the station managers from across the country to fly to company headquarters for a meeting. Then he made sure that every manager's luggage was lost in transit.

The result? You guessed it. The airline suddenly had a huge leap of progress in curtailing the problem of lost luggage.

And it was all because the airline's personnel instantly saw the problem from their customers' point of view.

When you accurately see any situation from another's point of view, when you can experience it like they do, you instantly take a different approach to it. We know that the word *instant* carries a strong promise, but it's true. Should we couch it by saying "almost instant"? We don't think so. Empathy can change everything in a moment. The moment you see a predicament from another's angle, once you have put yourself thoroughly in his or her shoes, you change—that very instant.

Just like the station managers for American Airways, you won't have to be goaded and pressured to make changes. You'll make the changes without further prodding. That's the promise of fast-acting empathy.

But maybe you need a little more convincing. Maybe you've been told that empathy takes too long. If so, allow us to underscore just how quickly empathy works.

Think of any convoluted conversation you've ever had— with a friend, a colleague, or even your spouse. Maybe it was a misunderstanding about a prescription. Perhaps it involved misread motivations concerning a joke in front of friends. Or maybe it was a lack of appreciation that caused you to clam up. Whatever the problem, wouldn't you like a way to make it immediately disappear? Wouldn't you like a magic button that would suddenly make things better? Sure. Who wouldn't? Well, that's what empathy can do.

It's quick.

As you're about to see, empathy does not require a long, drawn-out conversation to get things back on track. It can literally happen in an instant. For example, we recently had a conversation that became increasingly heated. It involved what to serve for a dinner party we were hosting in our home.

"You can just do enchiladas," Les asserted. "People love those."

"I'm not serving enchiladas," I protested. "These people are expecting a nice dinner."

"Well, then I don't know what to say." Les shrugged and left the room.

"Where are you going?" I shouted.

"I've got ice cream out on the counter in the kitchen," he hollered back.

I followed him into the kitchen and he could feel me gearing up for a hardheaded discourse on why enchiladas were not appropriate for the party and how he needed to be invested in this event as much as I was.

Before we made it to the softening ice cream, Les turned to me, put his hands on my shoulders, and said, "Help me see this from your side."

That's all it took. In less than a minute I told him how I had a limited amount of time to choose a menu, make the food, get the house ready, arrange for childcare, prep one of

> Nothing said to us . . . reaches us so deep as that which we find in ourselves.
>
> —THEODOR REIK

our sons for a spelling test, take my mom to a doctor's appointment, and so on.

"No wonder you're feeling frazzled," Les confessed. "I didn't realize all you had on your plate."

That was it. In a moment's time, Les suddenly saw my world from my perspective, and the tension melted long before his ice cream. He offered to take a few of my tasks, and we moved forward. The point is that without empathy our enchilada exchange would have devolved into an emotional and time-consuming upheaval that neither of us wanted.

You get the point. So don't let anyone tell you empathy is time consuming. It's not. Nothing works faster than empathy.

By the way, studies in the medical field have underscored the efficiency of empathy. More and more doctors are learning its expedient value. Why? Because it affects their bottom line. Physicians, of course, need to sense the anxiety and discomfort of their patients so they can treat them effectively. But they rarely "take the time" to do so. Believing it will slow them down, most physicians speed through their appointments without practicing much empathy. In fact, one study reveals that patients usually had an average of four questions in mind to ask, but during the visits they were

> We've all heard the criticism "he talks too much." When was the last time you heard someone criticized for listening too much?
>
> —NORM AUGUSTINE

able to ask just one or two. Once a patient started speaking, the first interruption by the physician occurred, on average, within eighteen seconds.

Physicians who trade places with their patients, on the other hand, tell their patients what to expect from a treatment, and they check in to be sure their patients understand what's happening. Incidentally, the lack of empathy is a primary predictor in malpractice lawsuits. And the time needed for a doctor to be successfully empathic? Just three minutes.

We'll say it again: nothing works faster than empathy.

Priming the Pump for Empathy

If you want to put empathy into practice, you've got to become a master at setting aside your personal agenda, if only momentarily. What is your agenda? It's nothing more than your set of immediate goals. That includes what you want to do (finish this chapter, decide on dinner plans, take a walk), what you want to feel (enlightened, challenged, superior), and what you want to talk about (a vacation, a challenge at work, how you felt hurt last night).

Your personal agenda is continually updated and revised. And it's a powerful force. It compels you to keep focused on your goal. Like an executive running a high-powered board meeting, you don't want to veer away from your agenda, because it means you may not reach your goal. The difference, of course, is that your agenda is not printed for distribution to family and friends. Sometimes your agenda remains unspoken. Sometimes, nobody knows it but you.

At other times, your agenda is often straightforward and out in the open. It may be an intensely emotional message that you want to get across. It's not disguised or cloaked in mystery. For example, you may want your spouse or a friend to know you're angry. You may want them to know that you won't stand for being belittled. And what happened earlier in the evening is something you don't want to ever happen again. In fact, you want them to pay a price for having embarrassed you. What do you do? You raise your voice, you pace around the room, you point your finger, and you induce guilt. Or maybe you clam up and retreat to another part of the house to get your message through. The point is, you will do whatever you can to accomplish your agenda. And the last thing you want to do when your agenda is red hot is set it aside.

But your agenda doesn't have to be an intense and emotional message you want to get across. It may just be talking on your phone or checking on a message. Whatever the task, your presence for another person becomes blunted whenever you split your focus. "A five-minute conversation can be a perfectly meaningful human moment," an article in the *Harvard*

> When empathy speaks up, it takes away stupidity's microphone.
>
> —UNKNOWN

Business Review notes. "To make it work, you have to set aside what you are doing, put down the memo you were reading, disengage from your laptop, abandon your day-dream, and focus on the person you're with."

Wherever your personal agenda item falls on the continuum from hot to cold, you have to set it aside if you want to practice empathy.

The Art of Empathy

Angela teetered as she walked across a medical conference room, thighs chafing, sweat glands sweating. She tried to squeeze into a regular-size chair, but her lumpy hips snagged on the arms. She moved to an extra-wide armless chair, but then she couldn't cross her plumped-out legs.

A dietitian helped her climb aboard a stationary bicycle that had been fitted with an oversized seat. But when Angela tried to pedal, thick, doughy rolls of abdominal tissue pressed against her thighs, impeding movement.

"Every move I made was an effort," Angela, thirty-five, later admitted. By then, however, she was slimmed down to her actual weight: 110 pounds.

Angela had been zipped into a bulky beige "empathy suit," designed to help medical personnel better understand the plight of their obese patients. The suit weighs only thirty pounds, but it feels heavier and effectively blimps out small low-body-fat people like Angela. Its sheer heft and bulk are intended to give them a new, deepened understanding of the workaday world of the obese.

Does it work? You bet. Angela saw firsthand that even a simple movement such as walking may be challenging for the obese. Having worn the suit, "[I] feel more respectful, more aware of their feelings," she says.

That's the power of self-giving love—putting oneself in the skin of another. Take any profession—teaching second graders, for example. You can improve a teacher's effectiveness by having her walk through her classroom on her knees. As she sees that space from a second-grader's perspective, she will naturally be better equipped to teach them. Or how about serving fast food? The major chains spend bundles of money sending "fake customers" into their stores to see it as they do. Advertising firms on Madison Avenue make their living by putting themselves in the consumer's shoes. Growing churches are expanding because they study the experience of a first-time visitor, and the pastor imagines what it is like to sit in the pew. Disneyland's "cast members" know that guests will average sixty contact opportunities in a single day at their theme park, and they want to make each of them a magic moment; so they continually work at empathizing with

> Yet, taught by time,
> my heart has learned
> to glow for others'
> good, and melt
> at others' woe.
>
> —HOMER

families. And, of course, a counselor wouldn't last a day without practicing empathy. How well we know!

The point is that empathy—the ability to accurately see the world through another's eyes—is at the heart of true understanding and the ability to extend self-giving love. Whether it's in medicine, business, education, or entertainment, empathy is a major determiner of success. More important, when it comes to our most important relationships, empathy is essential. Without empathy, healthy relationships are impossible. Self-giving love is null and void.

Consider your contentment when another person senses what you are feeling without you having to explain. This is the essence of empathy. While we can have interesting conversations and smooth social exchanges without it, we will never enter the inner chambers of a person's heart without empathy. It is the key to unlocking a person's spirit at the most intimate and vulnerable levels.

> If there is any one secret of success, it lies in the ability to get the other person's point of view and see things from that person's angle as well as from your own.
>
> —HENRY FORD

If asking a string of quality questions (that is, reading your social barometer from the previous chapter) is the equivalent of a BA in relationships, empathy will earn you your PhD in the social arts. Empathy is evidence of relational brilliance.

In 1990 psychologist Peter Salovey, now president of Yale

University, and the University of New Hampshire's psychology professor John Mayer coined the phrase "emotional intelligence" to describe qualities that bring human interactions to their peak of performance. Psychologist and *New York Times* science journalist Daniel Goleman brought the phrase into the national conversation with his groundbreaking book on the subject. He calls empathy our social radar and believes it operates at different levels. At the very least, empathy enables us to read another's emotions.

The key to identifying and understanding another person's emotional terrain, experts agree, is an intimate familiarity with one's own. Goleman cites the research of Robert Levenson at UC Berkeley as a prime example. Levenson brings married couples into his physiology lab for two discussions: a neutral talk about their day and a fifteen-minute emotionally charged discussion concerning a disagreement. Levenson records the husband's and wife's heart rates, muscle tension, changes in facial expressions, and so on. After the disagreement, one partner leaves. A replay of the talk is then narrated by the other partner, noting feelings on their end that were not expressed. Then the roles are reversed and that partner leaves, allowing the other person to narrate the same scene from his or her partner's perspective.

This is where researchers found something extraordinary. Partners adept at empathizing were seen to mimic their partner's body language while they empathized. If the heart rate of the partner in the videotape went up, so did the heart rate of the partner who was empathizing; if the partner's heart rate slowed down, so did that of the empathic spouse. This phenomenon, called *entrainment*, demands we put aside our own emotional agendas for the time being to clearly receive the other person's signals. As Goleman said, "When we are caught up in our own strong emotions, we are off on a different physiological vector, impervious to the more subtle cues that allow rapport."

Putting aside our own emotional agenda for empathy's sake brings us back to the question we posed in the previous chapter: What races through your head when you walk into a room of people? If you are not quietly asking yourself *How are these people doing?* you will never provide the psychological space for empathy to do its work. But when you do, you will begin to enjoy relational connections at a depth you never knew was possible.

> You will find as you look back upon your life that the moments . . . when you have really lived, are the moments when you have done things in a spirit of love.
>
> —HENRY DRUMMOND

Remember This

It will never rain roses: when we want to
have roses, we must plant more roses.

—GEORGE ELIOT

Do you remember the single sentence we gave you in the introduction of this book? It's the sentence that everything we've written about comes back to. Here it is again:

If you try to build intimacy with another before you have gotten whole on your own, all your relationships become an attempt to complete yourself.

At this point, after reading about how to get a lock on your profound significance (through better self-talk and moving past your past), unswerving authenticity (by discovering your blind spots and facing your fears), and self-giving love (by reading your social barometer and practicing empathy), we hope this sentence is more meaningful than ever. Like we said at the outset, if its truth can sink into your cortex and be lived out through your spirit, you and your relationships will become stronger than they have ever been.

Recently, when lecturing on relationship to about two hundred college students, we gave them this sentence and spent the class period unpacking it. Two weeks later a student approached us near the podium at the beginning of the class.

"Hey, Dr. Parrott?"

We were both gathering our notes and fiddling with some technology equipment for the lecture we were about to give.

"Yes, what is it?" Les replied.

"I wondered if I could have your attention."

"Sure," Les said, still focused on squaring away his notes.

"Well, I kind of need you to look at me," the student said.

That's when both of us put down everything we were doing and turned to give this student our full attention: "Okay. Yes. What can we do for you?" Les asked.

"You know on the first night of class when you gave us that important sentence?"

"Of course."

"Well, that was really meaningful to me. In fact, I don't ever want to forget it."

"Hey, that's fantastic, man," said Les. "I'm glad you enjoyed the lecture."

"No," the student continued. "It was *really* meaningful. Can I show you?"

We were both confused. What did he want to show us?

"Um. Okay."

At that point, the student lifted up part of his T-shirt to reveal a tattoo on the side of his ribcage. Sure enough. It was our sentence.

"Whoa!" Leslie exclaimed. "I didn't see that coming."

Part of us wanted to say, *Really? It's a good sentence. But a tattoo?*

Truth be told, we obviously don't need you to physically tattoo the sentence on your body to take the message of this book with you. But we hope, in a sense, that you'll tattoo it on your brain. We hope the message is getting into your being and you're taking it with you as you close the back cover of this book.

With that in mind, allow us to leave you, more specifically, with three points of hope surrounding your relationships. The first has to do with your relationship to God, the second with your relationship to yourself, and the third with your relationship to everyone else.

Profound Significance Relates to God

Most of us believe that our significance has to be earned. We try desperately to gain others' respect and admiration by working to *achieve* it. We work long hours to accomplish more so we can make more money or earn a better promotion, thinking these kinds of things will win us the acceptance and approval we crave. We think our achievements will make us more valuable. We think our net worth will bolster our self-worth. And it may, for a while. But no matter how hard we try and how much we achieve, our significance will never truly last until we replace our achieving with *receiving*.

The message of this entire book is lost on you if you don't realize that your profound significance—the kind that abides—is never earned. It's experienced. And the only way to experience it is by relating to God. The more you get to know your Creator, the more you receive God's love—God's incalculable love:

> I ask him that with both feet planted firmly on love, you'll be able to take in with all followers of Jesus the extravagant dimensions of Christ's love. Reach out and experience the breadth! Test its length! Plumb the depths! Rise to the heights! Live full lives, full in the fullness of God. (Eph. 3:17–19)

When this love is experienced deep in your bones, you'll discover that you're no longer spinning your wheels in a futile quest to prove how significant you are. You realize that no matter what you achieve—or what you don't—God loves you as if you're the only person on the planet to love.

The more you walk with God, the more you experience God's love. You may achieve as much as ever, maybe more, but your significance will no longer hang on the temporary feelings of achievement.

Your relationship with God is the starting place. It's where your journey toward health and wholeness begins. And once you get a lock on this one, it leads to another important relationship.

Unswerving Authenticity Relates to Yourself

Once you begin a serious relationship with God, where you are experiencing love from your Creator, you're ready to cultivate a healthier relationship with yourself. And there is only one way to get linked to your *best self* in a healthy way. It comes down to becoming unswervingly authentic. And that means following the path God called you to travel:

> I want you to get out there and walk—better yet, run!—on the road God called you to travel. I don't want any of you sitting around on your hands. I don't want anyone strolling off, down some path that goes nowhere. (Eph. 4:1–2)

In spite of what anyone thinks or says, the healthy person knows their purpose. They know the path God called them to travel and they aren't about to step off of it. They're no longer susceptible to the proverbial "disease to please." They are true to what they know God wants for them. They've given up on the notion of trying to be what others want and, instead, embrace who they are and what they want to become.

Shakespeare put it this way: "And it must follow, as the night the day, thou canst not then be false to any man." In other words, as you live authentically on a moment-by-moment basis, you become deeply linked to the true you. And it is the living out of this true you that puts you in sync with your purpose and your best self.

Self-Giving Love Relates to Others

Once you receive an abiding sense of significance, and once you travel the path you know you need to travel, you arrive at a place where your relationships transform. Whether it's with family, relatives, friends, colleagues, acquaintances, strangers, or even enemies, you are in a new place where love becomes your language. When you travel these steps, you will experience what Paul says:

> Pouring yourselves out for each other in acts of love, alert at noticing differences and quick at mending fences. (Eph. 4:3)

Empathy will come easier and compel you to see beyond petty slights and even deeper wounds that trip others up in their relationships. You'll find yourself sidestepping the kinds of disappointments, conflicts, and confusion that entangle so many in their relationships. Why? Because you're no longer consumed with you. You have new vision that sees others in ways that most don't. Where others see anger, for example, you'll see pain. The love and grace you're receiving from your Creator will spill over into all other relationships. You will find yourself giving yourself away, and your relationships will never be the same.

Acknowledgments

We are grateful to everyone who had a hand in helping us with this project.

First and foremost is our incredible publishing team at HarperCollins: Joey Paul, Webster Younce, Brigitta Nortker, Jamie Lockard, Stephanie Tresner, and Shea Nolan. Each of you is a delight to work with and the value you've added at every stage of this process is immeasurable.

Sealy Yates, who is not only a good friend but a great agent, is so entwined in our literary efforts at this point that we can't imagine doing this without him. A million thanks, Sealy, as always.

We are also indebted to long-time friend, Neil Clark Warren, for helping us hammer out many of the concepts in this book. Your friendship and wisdom over the years is simply a gift and we are forever grateful to you and Marylyn.

Our elite tactical team through this project (not to mention nearly everything else we do these days) includes Halie Simonds, Ryan Farmer, Kevin Small, and Ranjy Thomas. We could never do what we do without you. Each of you offers unparalleled competence and extraordinary dedication to our mission. While writing this book, you joined us for the wild ride of "Project Bluejay" and because of that we are forever linked together. And we will never be able to say thanks enough—for everything.

Notes

Introduction

xiii. "Wholeness does not mean": Parker J. Palmer, *A Hidden Wholeness: The Journey Toward an Undivided Life* (San Francisco: Jossey-Bass, 2008), 5.

xv. "I will no longer act": Quoted in Parker J. Palmer, *Let Your Life Speak: Listening to the Voice of Vocation* (San Francisco: Jossey-Bass, 2000), 33.

xviii. "Life is deep and simple": Les Parrott and Leslie Parrott, *The One Year Love Talk Devotional for Couples* (Carol Stream, IL: Tyndale, 2011), s.v. "November 5."

xviii. "There is no fool": Cicero, *The Academic Questions, Treatise De Finibus, and Tusculan Disputations of M. T. Cicero*, trans. C. D. Yonge (London: Henry G. Bohn, 1853), 120.

xviii. "The Bible says the same": The book of Psalms is filled with these life-affirming principles.

xviii. "When we are not honest": Clark E. Moustakas, *Being-In, Being-For, Being-With* (Northvale, NJ: Jason Aronson, 1995), 167.

xxi. "If thou wishest": Seneca, quoted in Craufurd Tait Rammage, *Great Thoughts from Latin Authors*, 3rd ed. (New York: John B. Alden, 1891), 550.

xxiii. "Destiny is not a matter": William Jennings Bryan, "America's Mission" (speech, Virginia Democratic Association, Washington, DC, February 22, 1899).

xxv.   "In a very simple experiment": Ellen Langer and Judith Rodin, "The Effects of Choice and Enhanced Personal Responsibility for the Age: A Field Experiment in an Institutional Setting," *Journal of Personality and Social Psychology* 34 (1976): 191–98.

xxv.   "Those who perceived themselves": James H. Johnson and Irwin G. Sarason, "Life Stress, Depression and Anxiety: Internal-External Control As a Moderator Variable," *Journal of Psychosomatic Research* 22 (1978): 205–8.

xxv.   "The difficulty in life": George Moore, *The Bending of the Bough: A Comedy in Five Acts* (London: T. Fisher Unwin, 1900), act IV.

xxvii. "It is not enough": Douglas Malcolm White, *Vance Havner, Journey from Jugtown: A Biography* (Old Tappan, NJ: Revell, 1977), 137.

xxviii. "People are anxious": James Allen, *As You Think: A New Thought Classic for Today's Woman* (Morrisville, NC: Lulu Press, 2014).

xxviii. "Your life is like a coin": Luis Palau, *High Definition Life: Trading Life's Good for God's Best* (Ada, MI: Revell, 2005), 15.

Part One: Profound Significance

4.   "Even if we agree": Ed Diener et al., "Subjective Well-Being: Three Decades of Progress," *Psychological Bulletin* 125 (1999): 276–302.

5.   "Ultimately, we find": Michael Argyle, "Causes and Correlates of Happiness," in *Well Being: The Foundations of Hedonic Psychology*, ed. Daniel Kahneman, Ed Diener, and Norbert Schwarz (New York: Russell Sage Foundation, 2000).

7.   "However good you feel": Alice M. Isen, Andrew S. Rosenzweig, and Mark J. Young, "The Influence of Positive Affect on Clinical Problem Solving," *Medical Decision Making* 11 (1991): 221–27.

Chapter 1: Tuning In to Your Self-Talk

14. "Healthy people are keenly": Alan Morin and James Everett, "Inner Speech as a Mediator of Self-Awareness, Self-Consciousness, and Self-Knowledge," *New Ideas in Psychology* 8 (1990): 337–56.

16. "Today the estimate": Suzana Herculano-Houzel, "The Human Brain in Numbers: A Linearly Scaled-Up Primate Brain," *Frontiers in Human Neuroscience* 3, no. 31 (2009), doi:10.3389/neuro.09.031.2009.

16. "I think, therefore": René Descartes, *Discourse on the Method* (1637).

17. "The brain is a circuitry": Barbara Hoberman Levine, *Your Body Believes Every Word You Say: The Language of the Body/Mind Connection* (Boulder Creek, CA: Aslan, 1991).

17. "And, over time, the secret": Sandra Blakeslee, "Tracing the Brain's Pathways for Linking Emotion and Reason," *New York Times*, December 6, 1994, B1.

19. "So he gave up psychoanalysis": Burkhard Hoellen, "An Interview with Albert Ellis," *Psychotherapy in Private Practice* 4 (2008): 81–89.

20. "It is often composed": Chris P. Neck and Charles C. Manz, "Thought Self-Leadership: The Influence of Self-Talk and Mental Imagery on Performance," *Journal of Organizational Behavior* 13 (1992): 681–99.

20. "Feelings are simply": Charles T. Brown and Paul W. Keller, *Monologue to Dialogue: An Exploration of Interpersonal Communication* (Upper Saddle River, NJ: Prentice-Hall, 1979), 8.

22. "We act upon our thoughts": Wayne Dyer, *You'll See It When You Believe It* (New York: Willliam Morrow, 2011), 124.

23. "Research suggests that you talk": Linda and Charlie Bloom, "Self-Talk: Don't Talk Mean to Yourself," *Psychology Today*, January 29, 2019, https://psychologytoday.com/ca/blog/stronger-the-broken-places/201901/self-talk.

24. "It definitively shows": Thomas M. Brinthaupt et al., "Assessing the Accuracy of Self-Reported Self-Talk," *Frontiers in Psychology* 6 (2015): 570–601.

24. "Abundant medical research has proven": Howard M. Shapiro, *The Power of Hope: A Doctor's Perspective* (New Haven, CT: Yale University Press, 1998).

24. "The impact of self-talk": Two seminal works that thoroughly document these studies are Albert Ellis, *Reason and Emotion in Psychotherapy* (New York: Stuart, 1962); and Aaron T. Beck et al., *Cognitive Therapy of Depression: A Treatment Manual* (New York: Guilford, 1979). In addition, Albert Bandura's article "Self-Efficacy: Toward a Unifying Theory of Behavioral Change" (*Psychological Review* 84 [1977]: 191–215) greatly strengthened the foundation for this thinking.

33. "In a landmark study": Manasseh N. Iroegbu, "Self Efficacy and Work Performance: A Theoretical Framework of Albert Bandura's Model, Review of Findings, Implications and Directions for Future Research," *Psychology and Behavioral Sciences* 4 (2015): 170–73.

33. "Until you value yourself": M. Scott Peck, *What to Do Between Birth and Death* (New York: William B. Morrow, 1992), quoted in John C. Maxwell, *The 360 Degree Leader: Developing Your Influence from Anywhere in the Organization* (Nashville: Thomas Nelson, 2011), 88.

34. "Most often this vicious": Ruth D. Grainger, "The Use and Abuse of Negative Thinking," *American Journal of Nursing* 91 (1991): 13–14.

34. "And according to some experts": Shad Helmstetter, *What to Say When You Talk to Yourself* (New York: Park Avenue Press, 2011), 33.

36. "You'll need more than inspiration": Research has found that reading a motivational quote can trigger the reward system in the brain to make you feel good by releasing endorphins that you haven't earned, and that temporary satisfaction can

actually make you less likely to get on with the task at hand. Even worse, you may feel guilty for not being more optimistic. You may feel bad because you haven't done anything in recent memory to become great.

36. "[The Christian] does not think": C. S. Lewis, *Mere Christianity* (repr., New York: HarperOne, 2015), 63.

36. "It may be helpful": Lawrence E. Williams et al., "The Unconscious Regulation of Emotion: Nonconscious Reappraisal Goals Modulate Emotional Reactivity," *Emotion* 9 (2009): 847–54.

37. "Because, as French philosopher": Blaise Pascal, *Pensées* (New York: Penguin Books, 1966), 75.

38. "In the 1700s, Jonathan Edwards": Jonathan Edwards, "A Divine and Supernatural Light, Immediately Imparted to the Soul by the Spirit of God, Shown to Be Both Scriptural and Rational Doctrine," sermon preached at Northampton, 1734, online at http://www.ccel.org/e/edwards/sermons/supernatural_light.html.

38. "It's what John Wesley": John Wesley, *Journal of John Wesley*, online at https://www.ccel.org/ccel/wesley/journal.vi.ii.xvi.html.

38. "Pascal, who was a mathematician": Blaise Pascal, quoted in Colin Smith, "Feeling, Not Just Knowing, God's Love," Unlocking the Bible, September 27, 2018, https://unlockingthebible.org/2018/09/four-testimonies-feeling-gods-love/.

39. "One who has been touched": Philip Yancey, *What's So Amazing About Grace?* (Nashville: HarperCollins Christian Publishing, 2003), 89.

Chapter 2: Moving Past Your Past

45. "Yesterday is but today's": Kahlil Gibran, *The Prophet* (repr., New York: Penguin Classics, 2019), 70.

46. "At the University of Kansas": C. R. Snyder, Raymond L. Higgins, and Rita J. Stucky, *Excuses: Masquerades in Search of Grace* (New York: Wiley-Interscience, 1983). See also

Melvin L. Snyder et al., "Avoidance of the Handicapped: An Attributional Ambiguity Analysis," *Journal of Personality and Social Psychology* 37 (1979): 2, 297–306.

47. "The past is a foreign country": L. P. Hartley, *The Go-Between* (repr., New York: New York Review Books Classics, 2002), 17.

48. "Go forth to meet": Henry Wadsworth Longfellow, *Hyperion*, bk. 4 (1839), chap. 8.

49. "But after the exercise": James Pennebaker, "Title," *Journal of American Medical Association* (1999).

50. "Who controls the past": George Orwell, *1984* (repr., New York: Berkley, 1983), 197.

55. "Studies do not justify blaming": The best review and synthesis of this literature that we are aware of is found in Martin E. P. Seligman, *Authentic Happiness* (New York: Free Press, 2002). Seligman has masterfully consolidated many studies in this area. Here is a sampling: Rex Forehand, "Parental Divorce and Adolescent Maladjustment: Scientific Inquiry vs. Public Information," *Behavior Research and Therapy* 30 (1992): 319–28; George W. Brown and Tirril Harris, *Social Origins of Depression* (London: Tavistock, 1978); R. Galbraith, "Sibling Spacing and Intellectual Development: A Closer Look at the Confluence Models," *Developmental Psychology* 18 (1982): 151–73; Anne Clarke and Alan Clarke, *Early Experience: Myth and Evidence* (New York: Free Press, 1976); and Michael Rutter, "The Long-Term Effects of Early Experience," *Developmental Medicine and Child Neurology* 22 (1980): 800–815.

57. "Research suggests that it's far": See Claudia Kalb, "Pen, Paper, Power! Confessional Writing Can Be Good for You," *Newsweek*, April 26, 1999, https://www.newsweek.com/pen -paper-power-165028. Stephen Lepore, an associate professor of psychology at Carnegie Mellon University, found that students who wrote expressively about their emotions before an exam had the same number of intrusive thoughts as those who wrote about superficial things. But they reported fewer

symptoms of distress. Lepore believes their worries about the
test simply became less disturbing.

57. "Realize that if you have time": Anthony J. D'Angelo, *The
College Blue Book: A Few Thoughts, Reflections & Reminders
on How to Get the Most Out of College & Life* (New York:
Arkad Press, 1995), 81.

58. "Summarizing a University of Michigan": Reed Larson, "Is
Feeling 'In Control' Related to Happiness in Daily Life?"
Psychological Reports 64 (1989): 775–84.

Part Two: Unswerving Authenticity

61. "Real isn't how you were made": Margery Williams, *The
Velveteen Rabbit* (New York: Macmillan, 1983), 4.

62. "We're afraid of being seen": Barbara Fredrickson, "The
Role of Positive Emotions in Positive Psychology: The
Broaden-and-Build Theory of Positive Emotions," *American
Psychologist* 56 (2001): 218–26.

62. "And he understood that sawdust": Williams, *Velveteen
Rabbit*, 3.

63. "making one's own wounds": Henri Nouwen, *The Wounded
Healer* (New York: Image Books, 1979), 88.

64. "He considered it a major requirement": A. H. Maslow, "A
Theory of Human Motivation," *Psychological Review* 50, no. 4
(1943): 370–96.

64. "Our thoughts, feelings, words, and actions": A. H. Maslow,
"A Theory of Human Motivation," *Psychological Review* 50,
no. 4 (1943): 370–96.

Chapter 3: Uncovering Your Blind Spots

67. "Research shows that we don't know": Robert Sternberg,
ed., *Why Smart People Can Be So Stupid* (New Haven: Yale
University Press, 2002).

69. "Knowing thyself is a way": Natalie Angier, "Evolutionary
Necessity or Glorious Accident? Biologists Ponder the Self,"

New York Times, April 22, 1997, https://www.nytimes.com
/1997/04/22/science/evolutionary-necessity-or-glorious
-accident-biologists-ponder-the-self.html.

70. "The unexamined life": Plato, *Plato in Twelve Volumes*, vol.
1: *Apology*, trans. Harold North Fowler (Cambridge, MA:
Harvard University Press, 1996), sec. 38a, accessed at Perseus
Digital Library, http://www.perseus.tufts.edu/hopper/text?doc
=plat.+apol.+38a.

70. "Reality is the leading cause": Lily Tomlin as Trudy in Jane
Wagner, *The Search for Signs of Intelligent Life in the Universe*,
rev. ed. (New York: Harper Perennial, 1991), 18.

73. "Oh, would [God] the gift": Updated English from Robert
Burns, "To a Louse" (1786), accessed at Robert Burns
Country, http://www.robertburns.org/works/97.shtml.

75. "In a comparison of executives": Morgan W. McCall and
Michael M. Lombardo, *Off the Track: Why and How Successful
Executives Get Derailed*, Technical Report no. 21 (Greensboro,
NC: Center for Creative Leadership, 1987).

75. "accuracy in self-assessment": Daniel Goleman, *Working with
Emotional Intelligence*, (New York: Bantam, 1998), 64.

75. "Egoism": Joachim Krueger and Ross A. Mueller, "Unskilled,
Unaware, or Both? The Better-Than-Average Heuristic and
Statistical Regression Predict Errors in Estimates of Own
Performance," *Journal of Personality and Social Psychology* 82
(2002): 180–88.

75. "Some people simply cannot": Paul J. Silvia and T. Shelley
Duval, "Predicting the Interpersonal Targets of Self-Serving
Attributions," *Journal of Experimental Social Psychology* 37
(2001): 333–40.

76. "The greatest of faults": Thomas Carlyle, *On Heroes, Hero-Worship
& the Heroic in History* (New York: Wiley & Putnam, 1846), 42.

79. "Those viewers who were aware": Peter Salovey et al.,
"Emotional Attention, Clarity and Repair: Exploring
Emotional Intelligence Using the Trait Meta-Mood Scale," in

Emotion, Disclosure, and Health, ed. James W. Pennebaker (Washington, DC: American Psychological Press, 1995).

79. "Those who kept journals": Goleman, *Working with Emotional Intelligence*.

80. "He had not realized": Richard S. Lazarus, *Emotion and Adaptation* (Oxford: Oxford University Press, 1994), 18.

81. "Your paradigm is so intrinsic": Donella Meadows, *The Global Citizen* (Washington, DC: Island Press, 1991), 4.

82. "Let us resolve to be masters": John Fitzgerald Kennedy (speech, University of Maine, October 19, 1963), accessed at Papers of John F. Kennedy, Presidential Papers, https://www.jfklibrary.org /asset-viewer/archives/JFKPOF/047/JFKPOF-047-034.

83. "I understood for the first time": Oprah Winfrey, "What I Know for Sure," *O, The Oprah Magazine*, February 2002, 184.

84. "A second self": William Styron, *Darkness Visible: A Memoir of Madness* (New York: Vintage, 1992), 64.

85. "You can arrange mirrors": Paul J. Silvia and T. Sheley Duval, "Objective Self-Awareness Theory: Recent Progress and Enduring Problems," *Personality and Social Psychology Review* 5 (2001), 230–41.

85. "It holds great potential": Rostyslaw W. Robak, "Self-Definition in Psychotherapy: Is It Time to Revisit Self-Perception Theory?" *North American Journal of Psychology* 3 (2001), 529–34.

86. "Man's capacity to experience": Rollo May, *Psychology and the Human Dilemma* (New York: Van Nostrand, 1967), 9, quoted in Eugene Rae Harcum, *A Psychology of Freedom and Dignity: The Last Train to Survival* (Westport, CT: Praeger), 161.

86. "Though the man's eyes": Oliver Sacks, "To See and Not See," *New Yorker*, May 2, 1993, https://www.newyorker.com /magazine/1993/05/10/to-see-and-not-see.

Chapter 4: Facing Your Fears with Honesty

91. "In the early conditioning": Martin E. P. Seligman, *Helplessness: On Depression, Development, and Death* (San

Francisco: Freeman, 1975). See also S. F. Maier and Martin E. P. Seligman, "Learned Helplessness: Theory and Evidence," *Journal of Experimental Psychology General* 105 (1976): 2–46.

91. "Once people reach their late": National Opinion Research Council, "Trends: Is Life Exciting or Dull?" GSS Data Explorer through NORC at University of Chicago, https://gssdataexplorer .norc.org/trends/Gender%20&%20Marriage?measure=life &response=Exciting&breakdown=Age%C2%B0.

94. "Our life is composed": Anais Nin, *The Journals of Anais Nin*, vol. 4 (London: Owen, 1972), 40.

95. "If you hear a voice": Vincent van Gogh to Theo van Gogh, October 28, 1883, accessed at Van Gogh's Letters: Unabridged and Annotated, http://www.webexhibits.org/vangogh/letter /13/336.htm.

95. "If I had to do it over again": Nadine Stair, eighty-five-year-old patient of Bernie Siegel, facing death, as quoted in his *Peace, Love and Healing: Bodymind Communication and the Path to Self-Healing* (New York: Harper and Row, 1989), 245–46.

96. "Who reflects too much": Johann Friedrich von Schiller, *Wilhelm Tell* (1803), act 3, scene 1.

96. "You can live on bland food": Eileen Guder, *God, But I'm Bored!* (New York: Dell Books, 1974), 74.

97. "Obstacles cannot crush me": Leonardo da Vinci, *The Notebooks of Leonardo da Vinci*, vol. 1, trans. Edward John Poynter and Mrs. R. C. Bell, ed. Jean Paul Richter, chapter 10: *Studies and Sketches for Pictures and Decorations*, n682, accessed at https://en.wikisource.org/wiki/The_Notebooks _of_Leonardo_Da_Vinci/X.

97. "[Learned helplessness is]": Martin E. P. Seligman, *Learned Optimism: How to Change Your Mind and Life* (New York: Vintage, 2006), 15.

97. "There is no chance": Ella Wheeler Wilcox, "Will," in *Poetical Works of Ella Wheeler Wilcox* (Edinburgh: W. P. Nimo, 1917).

98. "Not only that, but the girls": Ellen de Lara, James Garbarino, and James M. Cooper, *An Educator's Guide to School-Based Interventions* (Belmont, CA: Wadsworth, 2003).

98. "We look to those extrinsic": Teresa M. Amabile and Mukti Khaire, "Creativity and the Role of the Leader," *Harvard Business Review* 86, no. 10 (October 2008), https://hbr.org /2008/10/creativity-and-the-role-of-the-leader.

99. "The 1949 class of Harvard Business": Marilyn Wellemeyer, "The Class the Dollars Fell On," *Fortune*, May 1974.

100. "Even among men for whom": Gail Sheehy, *Pathfinders: Overcoming the Crises of Adult Life and Finding Your Own Path to Well-Being* (New York: Morrow, 1981).

100. "Man cannot discover new oceans": By the way, risk-takers, those who are willing to expand their life beyond their comfort zone, share a particular discipline worth noting. They listen only selectively to their critics.

101. "Fortune befriends the bold": John Dryden, *The Works of John Dryden: In Verse and Prose, with a Life*, vol. 2 (New York: George Dearborn, 1836), 181.

102. "It is easy to be brave": Aesop, "The Wolf and the Kid," *Aesop's Fables*, accessed at Lit2Go, https://etc.usf.edu/lit2go/35/aesops -fables/689/the-wolf-and-the-kid/.

102. "Paradoxical Commandments": Kent M. Keith, *The Silent Revolution: Dynamic Leadership in the Student Council* (Cambridge, MA: Harvard Student Agencies, 1968), 8.

104. "Live daringly, boldly, fearlessly": Henry J. Kaiser, "How to Capture Life's Greatest Values," *Reader's Digest* 56 (January 1950): 18.

104. "Faith is taking the first step": Concept attributed to Martin Luther King Jr. by Marian Wright Edelman.

105. "Love like you'll never": Susanna Clark and Richard Leigh, "Come from the Heart," quoted in Fred R. Shapiro, *Yale Book of Quotations* (New Haven, CT: Yale University Press, 2006), 156.

Part Three: Self-Giving Love

109. "You have a life before you": Henry Drummond, *The Greatest Thing in the World and Other Addresses* (New York: Fleming H. Revell, 1891), accessed at https://www.gutenberg.org/files /16739/16739-h/16739-h.htm.

110. "Perhaps you are wondering": Jonathan Haidt, "The Emotional Dog and the Rational Tail: A Social Intuitionist Approach to Moral Judgment," *Psychological Review* 108 (2001): 814–34.

110. "Time stops when we lend": Martin E. P. Seligman, *Authentic Happiness* (New York: Free Press, 2002), 9.

110. "In the process of developing": The honest quandary about the tension of self-sacrifice and self-protection has captured many magnificent minds. Anders Nygren's classic book *Agape and Eros* contrasts "acquisitive desire," with "sacrificial giving." Nygren, *Agape and Eros* (Philadelphia: Westminster Press, 1953), 210. C. S. Lewis called eros "need-love" and agape "gift-love." Thousands of volumes have explored these dueling desires. Lewis, *The Four Loves* (New York: Houghton Mifflin Harcourt, 1991), 1–2.

112. "I knew from past years": Mary Ann Bird, "The Whisper Test," short story, accessed at Brian Charette, "On Compassion: The Whisper Test," Leader Helps, February 6, 2017, http:// leaderhelps.com/2017/02/06/on-compassion-the-whisper-test/.

Chapter 5: Reading Your Social Barometer

116. "Healthy people thrive": J. J. Campos and K. C. Barrett, "Toward a New Understanding of Emotions and Their Development," in *Emotions, Cognition, and Behavior*, ed. C. E. Izard, J. Kagan, and R. B. Zajonc (New York: Cambridge University Press, 1984), 229–63.

117. "The deepest principle": William James, *The Letters of William James*, vol. 2 (Boston: Atlantic Monthly Press, 1920), 33.

119. "Alternatively, when your": Vincent B. Van Hasselt et al., "Social Skill Assessment and Training for Children: An

Evaluative Review," *Behavior Research and Therapy* 17 (1979): 413–37.

120. "A person who has experience": Chris J. Boyatzis and Chitra Satyaprasad, "Children's Facial and Gestural Decoding and Encoding: Relations Between Skills and with Popularity," *Journal of Nonverbal Behavior* 18 (1994), 37–42.

120. "Not only do they listen": Paul Eckman and Wallace V. Friesen, *Unmasking the Face* (Englewood Cliffs, NJ: Prentice Hall, 1975).

120. "No one can make you feel": *Reader's Digest* 37 (September 1940): 84.

120. "the Profile of Nonverbal Sensitivity": Robert Rosenthal et al., *Sensitivity to Nonverbal Communication: The PONS Test* (Baltimore: Johns Hopkins University Press, 1979). See also Robert Rosenthal and Ralph L. Rosnow, *Essentials of Behavioral Research: Methods and Data Analysis* (New York: McGraw Hill, 1991).

121. "Reading one's social barometer": Frank M. Gresham, "Social Skills and Learning Disabilities: Causal, Concomitant, or Correlational?" *School Psychology Review* 21 (1992): 348–60.

122. "A person who is shut out": Mother Teresa (speech, National Prayer Breakfast, Washington, DC, February 3, 1994), accessed at C-SPAN, https://www.c-span.org/video/?c4618931/mother-teresa-speaks-abortion-1994-national-prayer-breakfast.

122. "In the misfortune of our best friends": Francois de La Rochefoucauld, *Maximes* (Paris: C. Barbin, 1665), no. 583, quoted in Immanuel Kant, *Religion Within the Bounds of Bare Reason* (Indianapolis: Hackett Publishing, 2009), 38.

123. "Most everyone has bouts of shyness": Mark S. Alfano, Thomas E. Joiner Jr., and Mark Perry, "Attributional Style: A Mediator of the Shyness-Depression Relationship," *Journal of Research in Personality* 28 (1994): 287–300.

124. "Harvard professor emeritus Jerome Kagan": Jerome Kagan, *The Nature of the Child* (New York: Basic Books, 1994), 106.

124. "There are many steps": Sarah R. Baker and Robert J.

Edelmann, "Is Social Phobia Related to Lack of Social Skill? Duration of Skill-Related Behaviors and Ratings of Behavioral Adequacy," *British Journal of Clinical Psychology* 41 (2002): 243–57.

125. "I can't give you the formula": Herbert Bayard Swope, quoted in John Simkin, "Herbert Bayard Swope," Spartacus Educational, last updated August 2014, https://spartacus-educational.com /USAswope.htm.

126. "He has achieved success": Bessie A. Stanley, "Success Is Service," *Emporia Gazette*, December 11, 1905, 2.

128. "The applause of a single": James Boswell, *Life of Samuel Johnson* (1791; repr., London: Pitman, 1907), 905, accessed at https:// archive.org/details/lifeofsamueljohn02boswuoft/page/904.

129. "If you sometimes endure": William Blackstone, *Commentaries on the Laws of England* (Oxford: Clarendon Press, 1765), introduction, sec. 2, accessed at https://avalon.law.yale.edu /18th_century/blackstone_intro.asp.

131. "Lonely people talking": Lillian Hellman, *The Autumn Garden: A Play in 3 Acts* (New York: Dramatists Play Service, 1952).

132. "Genuine relationships cannot possibly exist": Marcus Tullius Cicero, *Cicero's Offices* (London: J. M. Dent, 1953), 212.

133. "Now this does not mean": See Ephesians 4:5.

133. "Remove respect from friendship": Marcus Tullius Cicero, *Laelius: On Friendship* 21.81.

133. "No act of kindness": Aesop, "The Lion and the Mouse," *Aesop's Fables*.

134. "Better be a nettle": Ralph Waldo Emerson, *Emerson: Essays and Lectures* (New York: Library of America, 1983), 340.

135. "In each of my friends": C. S. Lewis, *The Four Loves* (New York: Houghton Mifflin Harcourt, 1991), 61.

135. "I never found the companion": Henry David Thoreau, *Walden* (Scotts Valley, CA: CreateSpace, 2018), 75, accessed at http://www.literaturepage.com/read/walden-104.html.

Chapter 6: Stepping into Another's Shoes

138. "'tappers or listeners'": L. Newton, "Overconfidence in the Communication of Intent: Heard and Unheard Melodies" (PhD dissertation, Stanford University, 1990).

138. "The heart has its reasons": Blaise Pascal, English translation of *Pensées* 2nd ed. (1670), 263, accessed at https://fr .wikisource.org/wiki/Page%3APascal_-_Pens%C3%A9es %2C_%C3%A9dition_de_Port-Royal%2C_1670.djvu/343.

140. "And a few years ago we wrote": If you want to take a deeper dive into the topic of empathy, you might start with our book *Trading Places: The Best Move You'll Ever Make in Your Marriage* (Nashville: Zondervan, 2008). Much of this chapter is drawn from our work in that book. And for a more scholarly read on the topic, we recommend Roman Krznaric, *Empathy: Why It Matters and How to Get It* (New York: Tarcher Perigee, 2015) as well as Helen Riess and Liz Neporent, *The Empathy Effect: Seven Neuroscience-Based Keys for Transforming the Way We Live, Love, Work and Connect Across Differences* (Boulder, CO: Sounds True, 2018).

141. "I do not ask how": Walt Whitman, *Leaves of Grass* (New York: Dover Publications, 2007), 50.

143. "I try to hear things": Ascribed to Leonard Riggio, founder and chairman of Barnes & Noble.

145. "The great gift of human beings": Michael Segell, "Get the Skinny on Streep," *Cosmopolitan* (May 1991), 197, accessed at Simply Streep, http://www.simplystreep.com/gallery/display image.php?album=480&pid=26023#top_display_media.

145. "In the study, researchers": Rachel A. Simmons, Peter C. Gordon, and Dianne L. Chambless, "Pronouns in Marital Interaction: What Do 'You' and 'I' Say About Marital Health?," *Psychological Science* 16 (2005): 932–36.

146. "To be as accident-prone": Bo Lozoff, *It's a Meaningful Life: It Just Takes Practice* (New York: Penguin, 2001), 24.

146. "It is only as we fully understand": S. I. Hayakawa, *Symbol, Status, and Personality* (New York: Houghton Mifflin, 1966), 35.

149. "the airline's personnel instantly saw": Cited in Kelly E. Middleton, *Competing for Kids: 21 Customer Service Concepts Public Schools Can Use to Retain and Attract Students* (Tucson, AZ: Wheatmark, 2018), concept 6.

150. "Nothing said to us": Theodor Reik, *The Search Within: The Inner Experiences of a Psychoanalyst* (New York: Farrar, Straus & Cudahy, 1956), 263.

151. "We've all heard the criticism": Norm Augustine, *Augustine's Laws* (New York: Viking, 1986).

152. "Once a patient started speaking": Howard B. Beckman and Richard M. Frankel, "The Effect of Physician Behavior on the Collection of Data," *Annals of Internal Medicine* 101 (1984): 692–98.

152. "Just three minutes": Wendy Levinson, "Physician-Patient Communication: The Relationship with Malpractice Claims Among Primary Care Physicians and Surgeons," *Journal of the American Medical Association* 277 (February 1997): 553–59.

153. "Sometimes, nobody knows": Sometimes you may not be fully aware of your own agenda without a serious look inward. That's where our unconscious agendas reside. These are the deep drives we have generated from unmet needs that started as early as childhood. Or they may be unconscious yearnings that were never met in a previous marriage. They could be unconscious desires from our dark side—things we don't even want to admit to ourselves, such as a hunger for attention or power. Of course, to bring these "agendas" to light you often need the help of a counselor or mentor.

154. "To make it work": Edward Hallowell, "The Human Moment at Work," *Harvard Business Review* (January–February 1999): 59.

155. "Its sheer heft and bulk": M. Voboril, "A Weighty Issue/Empathy Suit Shows Medical Personnel What It's Like to Be Obese," *Newsday*, April 16, 2000, B03.

155. "Yet, taught by time": Homer, *Odyssey*, bk. 18, line 279.

156. "Disneyland's 'cast members' know": Tom Connellan, *Inside the Magic Kingdom: Seven Keys to Disney's Success* (Austin, TX: Bard Press, 1997), 79.

157. "He calls empathy our social radar": Daniel Goleman, *Working with Emotional Intelligence* (New York: Bantam Books, 1998), 133.

157. "Goleman cites the research": Robert W. Levenson and Anna M. Ruef, "Physiological Aspects of Emotional Knowledge and Rapport," in William Ickes, ed., *Empathic Accuracy* (New York: Guilford Press, 1997), 44–72, cited in Goleman, *Working with Emotional Intelligence*, 135–36.

158. "When we are caught up": Goleman, *Working with Emotional Intelligence*, 136.

158. "You will find as you look": Henry Drummond, *The Greatest Thing in the World: Experience the Enduring Power of Love* (Ada, MI: Revell, 2011), 52.

Conclusion

164. "As the night the day": William Shakespeare, *Hamlet*, act 1, scene 3.

About the Authors

The #1 *New York Times* bestselling authors Drs. Les and Leslie Parrott are psychologists and founders of the game-changing online assessments: SYMBIS.com, BetterLove.com, and Yada.com. Their bestselling books include *Love Talk*, *The Good Fight*, *Crazy Good Sex*, and the award-winning *Saving Your Marriage Before It Starts*. Their work has been featured in the *New York Times* and *USA Today* and on CNN, *Good Morning America*, TODAY, *The View*, and *Oprah*. LesAndLeslie.com

You've read the book...
now make it stick!

Take a deeper dive into the most practical
parts of each chapter by visiting our
Healthy Me, Healthy Us blog.

You'll discover Les and Leslie's latest
wisdom, ideas, and advice on how to better
your relationships by bettering yourself.

HealthyMeHealthyUs.com

DISCOVER THE SCIENCE OF <u>YOU</u>

Yada is for everyone who wants to be the best version of themselves—and enjoy healthier, stronger and more fulfilling relationships.

The 10 power-packed pages of customized insights provide you with:

- A step by step process for realizing instant results
- Proven and reliable guidance you can count on
- An upbeat and encouraging tone for positive outcomes
- Engaging exercises and numerous conversation starters

In short, knowing yourself and those around you simply does not get better or easier than this.

Yada!

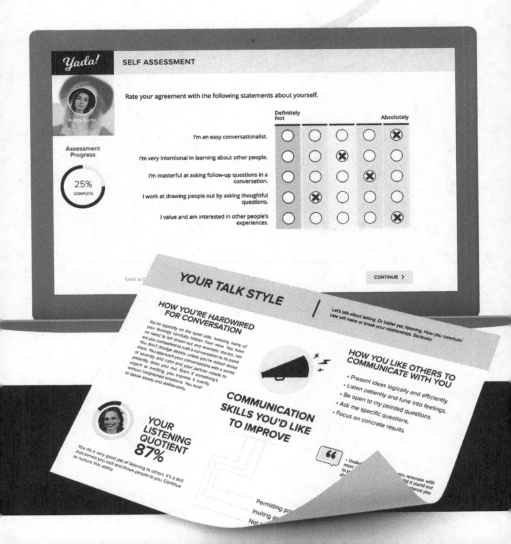